Home Stretch

Louis H. Potvin

Trafford
PUBLISHING®

Order this book online at www.trafford.com
or email orders@trafford.com

You may also email the author at carolou2@xplornet.com or at

HJ Developments Ltd.
Box 220, Pemberton, BC, Canada
V0N 2L0

Most Trafford titles are also available at major online book retailers.

Printed in the United States of America.

ISBN: 978-1-4907-1955-9 (sc)
978-1-4907-1954-2 (e)

Library of Congress Control Number: 2013922571

Trafford rev. 4/9/2014

Trafford
PUBLISHING® www.trafford.com
North America & international
toll-free: 1 888 232 4444 (USA & Canada)
fax: 812 355 4082

Contents

ACKNOWLEDGEMENTS

I could not have put this material together without the help of others. Carol scoured her well organized photo collection to meet the needs of HOME STRETCH. Marc St. Pierre our grandson helped get us started with his computer skills. Rosemary Morgan, PhD, our granddaughter in Edinburgh undertook the preparation and submission of the manuscript. Kurt Poetzschke worked day and night preparing collages adding colour to HOME STRETCH. Joanne Pollard of Altitude Computers kept our computers operating. And when we were exhausted our granddaughter Mireille St. Pierre organized what remained to be done. Writing my first book LOUIS PLACE with co-author Ron Rose was the impetus that gave me the confidence to embark on HOME STRETCH.

To all of you I express my appreciation for your help. To my wife Carol a special "Thank You" for your understanding and contribution in making this happen.

PREFACE

Let me tell you about myself Louis Potvin. My first book LOUIS' PLACE covered many years of my life. This book HOME STRETCH is a continuation of those earlier years. A school dropout having only finished grade 7 is not a recipe for future success. Looking back over my upbringing there was none in the normal sense. My parents had separated; my mother away working long hours left me alone to fend for myself while other kids where attending school. This left me exposed to the influence of many. My uncle, my grandparents and my mother's business partner who I would encounter frequently. I recall him telling me you can't just sit around you have to be a go getter. My exposure to my uncle, a carpenter, taught me how to build things. My grandparents, settlers in Alberta from Quebec, instilled in me love of family, being responsible, and that anything worth doing is to be done right. During all this I was exposed to French and English Canadian culture. It was only in the later years of my life did I come to appreciate the value of this influence.

The go getter instinct has developed into a small town entrepreneur. It is with reservations I refer to myself as an entrepreneur. I have sought for my own betterment and those of my family. Projects that would be of benefit to the community are what appealed to me. It was only when leaving the city corporate world to set out in untamed mountainous country at age 40 did the projects described in HOME STRETCH come into being. It is the get-up and go that got these projects started, but let me make it clear it did not all happen of my own doing. It took those in authority to see the benefit of a proposed project, friends along the way lending a helpful hand, and above all the support of my wife and business partner.

With all that said enjoy your read of HOME STRETCH.

CHAPTER 1: THE LAKE CALLS

How we came to own Lillooet Lake property is a story in itself. I had been flying up and down the British Columbia coast installing radiotelephones where there had never been any communication. This was in 1947 after receiving my discharge from the Royal Canadian Air force. Think of the thrill of being able to pick up a telephone in an isolated area, connect with the Vancouver Telephone Radio Operator and speak with your business people and loved ones. These experiences introduced me to many opportunities for the purchase of property. While land was available how would a young family make use of recreational property in these remote locations? Our company president Jim Spilsbury suggested exploring north of Garibaldi PGE rail station as there might be skiing areas there some day.

Head of Lillooet Lake where the Lillooet and Birkenhead Rivers empty into the lake. Lillooet Lake Road heading west to Mount Currie and Pemberton.

By chance I read an advertisement in the newspaper for Pemberton farm land. I responded by mail asking about the cost of few acres and for any possibilities of land by a stream, or better still by a lake, not expecting such property to be available. An interesting reply came by mail a copy of which follows.

Off we went by PGE train to Pemberton 98 miles from North Vancouver riding in the new Bud Car recently placed in operation. We disembarked at the Pemberton rail station with our two children, Heather age 9 and Bruce age 7. Remember Pemberton had no road access and to some degree was more like the Wild West. We walked across the dusty road towards the hotel amongst saddle horses and wagons to meet Mr. Taylor the sales agent with whom we had been corresponding. We were taken to his home at Taylor's corner. Refreshed and ready we took off for Lillooet Lake 14 miles away

I sat on a bouncy spare tire in the back of the pick-up truck and what a ride it was. Bumping along over ragged rocks on the edge of steep hillsides and clear drops into the Lake I made up my mind this place was not for me. The Hydro Transmission Line to Vancouver built a few years earlier was covered with unsightly debris. The whole area had been logged leaving skid trails and stumps. Not a pretty sight to see. Mr. Taylor unconcerned, said not to worry this will all grow back in time and be green once again.

Dealer Imperial Oil Company
at Pemberton Station
Contract Hauling — Taxi

Agents McCormick-Deering
International Harvester
Builders' Supplies

THE PEMBERTON EXPRESS

PROPRIETOR, R. H. E. TAYLOR

PEMBERTON, B.C. .... 19 ......   *25th April 1958*

Louis H Potvin.
4574 Belmont Ave.
Vancouver.

Dear Sir:-

Answering your letter of Apr 22nd, it so happens that I have a property situated 6 miles down Lillooet Lake on the best side of the Lake comprising 128 acres with 3/4 mile lake frontage and a stream flowing thru to the Lake.

The present road to it is O.K. in Summer but not kept open in Winter. The climate is exceedingly dry and warm and sof fruits do well, even to peaches altho I would not guarantee that to be a commercial venture. The land has been logged off but there are plenty of trees left and it could be converted into a beautiful homesite as time goes by. The present road runs from Harrison Lake at Pt Douglas to Pemberton. Someday it will doubtless be a highway but not for a few years. You could get to it now by car if you shipped by scow to Pt Douglas from Harrison Hot Springs, or you can come to Pemberton and drive to it from this end. Actuall it is much closer to this end.

We hope and expect a road will be built from Squamish to Pemberton, in fact there was a road there in 1898 and the present trail is passable to 4 wheel drive in the Summer and is used by B.C.E. maintainance crews on the powerline.

This property I have listed and the owner would accept $1500.00 perhaps a little less for all cash. It won't be there long, in fact I have half a mind to buy it for myself for a place to Sundays. The Lake is a cold lake but if you don't like cold water a swimming pool could be constructed at very little expense.

If your friend wanted something like it I can get the adjacent 128 acres north of this place but have to chase it up. At present there is little interest in these lands as the public are slow on the uptake, but I feel pretty sure that the time is almost here when the demmand will be obvious.

If you can come up please phone me in the evening at Pemb 1 B in order that I can be sure of being here when you arrive as I am away a good deal.

yours truly,

... Boost Your Interior Howe Sound Road and Railway

2

It was hot that May 10th 1958 day. The lake was a deep green, calm, quiet with the sound of tumbling water from a creek across the lake. The peaceful setting captivated us; our decision was soon made to purchase the property for the sum of $1,500, money we did not have. We were driven back to Pemberton. Business here required it be completed early in the same day if we were to board the train to Vancouver.

The photo of the Pemberton Express Garage shown on the next page is where our historic purchase took place. The arrow points to the carport where Mr. Taylor and I sat on chopping blocks and signed the purchase agreement. The terms were to be $500 down and two payments of $500 at six month intervals without interest. Mr. Taylor had agreed to pay the owner the sum of $750 for the property. The owner's wife insisted they receive the full payment of $750 otherwise the sale was off. Mr. Taylor was profiting from this sale at double the purchase price and therefore he should first come up with the cash. We set upon raising the purchase price ourselves. This involved cracking open our piggy bank and a loan from our regular bank. Little did we know this was to become our future home.

It was first a World War One soldier's grant of $10 in the year 1919. Now in 1958 it was being purchased by a city fellow for $1,500. The locals considered this property to be worthless after the ravages of the Transmission Line and logging operations. Living in a locked-in area with no road in or out did not expose the local residents to the thirst city dwellers had for rural land.

Mr. Taylor had at one time operated the company tug boat delivering supplies to the lake logging operation. This was a float camp tied up in front of the land now being offered. Years later a former worker at this camp informed me the tug broke away on a stormy night while the crew was absent and sank in the lake a short distance away where it still remains. Then it came to mind my earlier connection with this piece of land. The Hydro Transmission Line was the one I had supplied radio communications equipment for the construction crews to communicate to their base in Pemberton and other points for the BC Electric company. Later our company files revealed I had sold radio equipment to Fleetwood logging, the owners of the float camp on the DL-4901 property we were now inspecting. This equipment was for their communication link with the Vancouver Telephone Service and two way radio communications equipment for their logging operation along the shores of Lillooet Lake.

It is May 10, 1958, one of the hottest days of the year. The arrow points to Mr. Taylor's outdoor office where the paper work took place for the purchase of Lillooet Lake property. The Pemberton Express provided a much needed service in transporting goods, pumping gas, stocking automotive parts, and housing a First Aid Station. To the right is the community hall where on occasion bingo games and movies were held.

To have the good fortune to own property by a lake was a dream come true. As a boy in years 1933/36 I lived with my grandparents by a small lake on their farm in northern Alberta. Later when living in the Vancouver area I frequently boated in local waters increasing my love of being near water. Flying in and out of British Columbia coastal inlet waters installing radiotelephones increased my thirst for waterfront property. Lillooet Lake, long and narrow with towering mountains one each side reminded me of many coastal inlets I had visited. I felt at home here.

Before long we shipped up our 15 ft. Shasta trailer by rail flat car. Mr. Taylor our agent arranged for a bulldozer to tow our trailer down the lake by a young couple Earl Rivet and his wife Norma. It was a challenge getting this trailer to its new home. It was not long thereafter we constructed a 1500 square ft. home financed through the Veterans Land Act Assistance program. In year 1965 this became our main home. Moving into the area we embarked on several undertakings all well described in our book LOUIS PLACE.

We began receiving enquiries about purchasing lake shore property. The get up and go I had been taught as a youth came into play. Some call it the entrepreneurial spirit, some have said it is having a vision as to what can be done, to me it is the challenge of one's ability to complete the job. An opportunity in itself is not enough. It is what one does with that opportunity that counts. It is not profit alone that drives the entrepreneur.

We researched the possibility of creating a recreational community on the lake. A Land Use Contract was entered into with the newly formed Squamish Lillooet Regional District for a 177 site development. This involved satisfying the requirements of many government offices and undertaking challenges that were special to this project. Our plan received final approval by Order in Council by the British Columbia government. We pay tribute to the foresight of the Regional District directors of the day acknowledging the benefits that would accrue from this development.

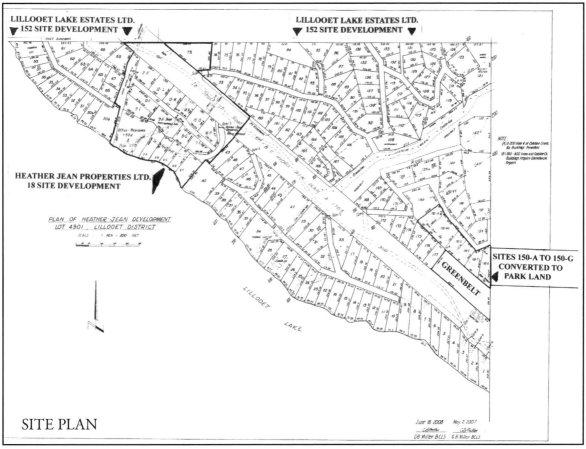

ORDER IN COUNCIL

M 18717

787   15:10

I hereby certify that the following is a true copy of a Minute of the Honourable the Executive Council of the Province of British Columbia approved by His Honour the Lieutenant-Governor.

APPROVED AND ORDERED   -3. MAR. 1977

W S Owen

_____
Assistant Deputy Provincial Secretary

_____
Lieutenant-Governor

EXECUTIVE COUNCIL CHAMBERS, VICTORIA   -3. MAR. 1977

Pursuant to the   Municipal   Act, and upon the recommendation of the undersigned, the Lieutenant-Governor, by and with the advice and consent of the Executive Council, orders that By-law No. 88 of the Squamish-Lillooet Regional District cited as "Land Use Contract Authorization By-law No. 88, 1976" be approved in the form of by-law hereto attached.

Minister of Municipal Affairs and Housing.

W. R. Bennett

Presiding Member of the Executive Council.

Slim Fougberg, Chairmen Squamish Lillooet Regional District.

Dan Cumming, Director of the Regional District.

Shirley Henry, Mayor of Pemberton and Director of the Regional District.

George Miller, British Columbia Land Surveyor.

WHAT A DIFFERENCE 125 TO 150 YEARS CAN MAKE

In the 1860's Lillooet lake was one of a chain of lakes leading to the British Columbia gold fields. The sternwheeler Prince of Wales plied Lillooet Lake transporting miners and mules on their way to Anderson and Seton Lakes and their fortune in the Quesnel area.

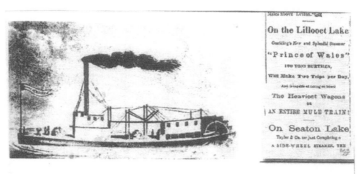

The Sternwheeler "Prince of Wales" that plied Lillooet Lake waters carrying fortune seekers on the first Gold Rush Trail to the Cariboo via Harrison, Lillooet, Anderson and Seton Lakes. The 100-ton Prince of Wales could accommodate an entire mule train or the heaviest wagons. The fare was $1.00 for the twenty mile trip from the Mile 29 stopping house to Port Pemberton at the head of the lake
Photo Credit: British Columbia Archives

Lower left: The houseboat Carolou tied up at Lizzie Bay down the lake. It has the same design of a gang plank for entering and disembarking as used by the Prince of Wales only 135 years later. Shown are grandchildren Mireille, Marc, daughter-in-law Aya with the family dog Daisy.

Lower right: Water skiing on Lillooet Lake, something not thought of in days gone by.

OPENING DAY FOR MOUNTAIN FM

After 1979 Carol and I had completed a number of projects I was asked if there was any other business enterprise we could start. My answer was a radio station serving Squamish, Whistler and Pemberton. Carol asked could you make it work? I answered yes, my radio communication background provided me with the technical skills required and what we did not know our entrepreneurial drive would come up with the answers. Traveling the highway to Vancouver we frequently encountered bad weather conditions, rock slides and bridge outages. Broadcasting news of the condition of the highway would be a public service. A killer highway it was becoming known as in the 1970's and early 1980's.

Before long we had a survey underway to determine what support there would be for local radio. The results were overwhelming in favour of such a project. We filed an application for broadcasting licenses with CRTC: the Canadian Radio Television Commission for Squamish, Whistler and Pemberton. This was followed with a public hearing. These three stations would all be programmed out of the Squamish studio. There was great excitement upon all three licenses being granted. The timing was right for us to embark on this undertaking. Carol and I had time for this new venture as the demand for properties at the lake had slowed down due to poor market conditions.

The launching of Mountain FM could not have come at a worse time. A severe recession was underway. The closing of the mill, the pulp mill in decline, businesses closing, as well as Whistler's difficulties lowered the general mood. The coming on air of Mountain FM Radio improved everyone's spirits.

Opening day in Squamish was a momentous affair. At 5:00 AM in the parking lot. I met the young lady DJ about to go on air. Broadcast school had not prepared her for such a moment. She was a very nervous young lady. I gave her big hug and told her I had confidence she would perform well. It went off without a hitch. Local listeners felt pride at hearing a radio voice in their community. The Mountain FM staff relaxed upon hearing the first words spoken on air: "GOOD MORNING THIS IS MOUNTAIN FM WITH THE LOCAL NEWS." I too felt more relaxed knowing all the equipment, cables and wiring had performed as expected. Our Program Director had gotten so keyed up making preparations for the opening day that he needed time away to recuperate. On such short notice I had to step up to the microphone and conduct the on air interviews. Before long the Program Director was back on the job the tension having worn off. Years of enjoyment at a microphone working the Radio Ham Bands and speaking with other Ham Operators all over the world had prepared me for a moment such as this.

In order to share with you some of the challenges in operating Mountain FM, we have included several photos of our activities. What we cannot show you is how hard everyone worked towards making this a success and survive during the recession. The downturn was felt by those who advertised with us resulting in many ingenious exchanges. In spite of this Mountain FM continued to grow. It was with great satisfaction when our on air programming assisted in the raising of funds for the hospital and other worthy causes.

OPENING NIGHT FOR MOUNTAIN FM IN SQUAMISH 1981

Top left: Squamish Mayor Jim Elliot cutting the ribbon. Sea to Sky guests looking on.

Lower right: Louis Potvin at the mic on opening night with Carol Potvin looking on.

Lower left: CISQ-FM Squamish transmitter site. Hydro pole line constructed to site. Fully equipped transmitter building flown in by jumbo helicopter.

A FEW PHOTOS OF WHAT IS INVOLVED IN OPERATING A RADIO STATION

David Larsen Program Director

Left: Mountain FM highway cruiser with Louis Potvin reporting to the studio via radio repeaters all before cell phones.

Right: To restore broadcasting helicopter transport was used in emergencies. Louis Potvin repair man about to take off.

Lower left: A Mountain FM promotion in Howe Sound for an advertiser.

Lower right: On air personality Diane Newman.

NOT ALL WORK AND NO PLAY

One of the practices in the broadcasting industry is the getting together of staff and advertisers. Working in this industry can be a fun thing; very much so at our time at Mountain FM where most of the employees were young and just out of broadcast school. Many were waiting to be discovered, sending out demo tapes to other larger stations. Many of our young people moved on to other larger markets both in radio and television. Our investors were invited to come along and meet the staff at Mountain FM. One such occasion is shown below on a fishing trip up the Howe Sound channel.

Fishing expedition up Howe Sound. Pemberton Mayor Shirley, husband George and Fred Wiley.

Carol Roycroft with the catch of the day. Carol was the Mountain FM accountant working long hours during difficult times.

NEW OWNERSHIP FOR MOUNTAIN FM RADIO

There comes a time to change course. Accepting an offer to purchase Mountain FM was exhilarating, a financial relief, and promise of a lightened workload. It was also a moment of sadness stepping out of the business that we had worked so hard to create. We accomplished what we set out to do in bringing in a much needed service to the community. It was not in the pecking order for us to have a broadcasting license for the Vancouver area.

The unsold sites at Lillooet Lake pledged to the Federal Business Bank carried us through difficult times with an interest rate reaching as high as 22%. We enjoyed a good working relationship with the Federal Business Development Bank (FBDB) even though it was said they would likely never be paid back. This doom and gloom thinking was prevalent during this severe recession. The fledgling Whistler ski resort was in the midst of a down turn with several businesses failing. It was with great pleasure I visited our local manager of the FBDB and was reminded of the bad loan the bank had made. I seized the moment to gently slip across his desk our cheque to the bank for the full payment covering our loans.

The photo below was taken in the purchaser's law office at the time all the dots and crosses were being attended to in the transfer of ownership for Mountain FM Radio. Seated clockwise is myself, Louis Potvin, President of Mountain FM, Carol Potvin Manager, the purchaser's Tom Peacock of Selkirk Broadcasting, their lawyer, and John Croft the lawyer acting for Mountain FM Radio.

LILLOOET LAKE IS CALLING

During our years at Mountain FM we were home at the lake on weekends. What little business there was we could attend to on those days. Returning to what we loved best was something we looked forward to. The 152 site owners had grown to where they were managing their own affairs, now known as Lillooet Lake Estates Ltd. After a bumpy start this group developed into a popular working community. We have included several of the cabins as well as some of those who occupy these homes within the book.

We have developed the remainder of our land into sites. An 18 site development was created known as Heather Jean Properties Ltd., much along the same lines as Lillooet Lake Estates Ltd. Each group as neighbours operate separately from one another. Our home and office is one of the 18 sites. Our story is about Lillooet Lake and an entrepreneur's project. The grandchildren have been included as the lake experience was part of their lives when growing up, especially during the 19 years the Carolou houseboat was on the lake. We have included chapters paying tribute to those we have worked and rubbed shoulders with, as well as friends who have shared our enthusiasm for life at the lake. There is mention of new friends of a more recent date who have assisted us in maintaining contact with clubs and the computer world. In conclusion, Home Stretch would not be a book by Louis Potvin without having borrowed quotations and philosophies from life.

Top photo: Scenic view at the lake. Communication towers on the right.

Lower photo: Lake shore facilities at Heather Jean Properties Ltd.

CHAPTER 2: MAKING SAWDUST

This is the story of the Potvin adventures in the sawmill business. It began in the 1970s when son Bruce became a sawyer for the large Evan's Forest Product mill in Pemberton. Bruce had chosen to MAKE SAWDUST in the expression of the day rather than continue his studies after completing high school. The Evan's Product stud mill closed after operating with poor quality logs and an uncertainty as to a future log supply.

The pressure was on to set up a sawmill and planer mill on our Lillooet Lake property. The idea seemed practical. Pemberton was home base for several logging operators. A log supply would be at our door and customers too, as new lot owners at the lake were eager to start on their dream cabins in the woods. The object of their desires, large rustic beams, would be available at the Lillooet Lake property. The expense of outside purchase and delivery over our primitive road far exceeded the budgets of bush pioneers.

Top photo: Heather Jean sawmill, Lillooet Lake spring1976. **Lower left photo:** Planer mill at Lillooet Lake, Peter Eisenbock student mill worker. **Lower right photo:** Product shown is a package produced by our Heather Jean mill

Our neighbours at the lake were delighted. A flurry of construction began once dimension lumber and the rustic beams became available. Word spread to the developing Whistler Ski Resort and beyond. Carol became the sales representative and before long we were loading tractor trailers of Lillooet Lake products destined for Vancouver lumber yards as well.

Our mill workers were a mix of young and older, male and female. In a short time with this lively mix we had acquired a new family member, daughter-in-law Lynn. Her keen sense of humour and formidable skills were a welcome addition to the family. She loaded and unloaded trucks, operated machinery and supervised workers, as Bruce made sawdust with Lynn running the yard and Carol on sales we had a winning combination. At the same time our family at the lake continued to grow as Lynn and Bruce produced grandchildren Renee and Kevin.

Top left photo: Lynn Potvin and Lynn Haskins piling lumber, Lillooet Lake sawmill.1970s. **Bottom left photo:** Eve Alvarez from Guatemala, sawmill cook. **Top right photo:** Lynn and Margo mixing cement. **Bottom right photo:** Louis Potvin with daughter-in-law Lynn.

Babies of course need attention. Renee entertained in the office and brother Kevin, bundled up, rode at his mother's feet while she operated the Patrick loader. Kevin loved the hum of the engine. To this day he is prone to falling asleep when riding as a passenger in a vehicle.

The lumber market called for graded products. Lynn answered the challenge and enrolled in the course for certification as a qualified lumber grader. She found herself the only woman in the group of rough, tough woodsmen not yet familiar with the concept of equal opportunity. Examination day came with numbered sample boards moving along a conveyor belt. The trick was to pick up a numbered board, grade it as to composition and quality and record your findings. As the conveyor with sample boards moved alongside the shoulder to shoulder line of burly woodsmen Lynn managed to elbow in and retrieve a board but not without difficulty. One fellow grabbed the board Lynn had selected. Only after determined tugging did she end up with her sample. The adjacent lumbermen stood back in amazement at this demand for equal rights.

Many of our mill crew were workers from the local Mount Currie Native Band. We provided an older vehicle, or crummy, for their use travelling back and forth to the mill. Others were city student workers subsidized by the government, housed and fed on our property. Being young they experienced problems with real life and frequently sought personal guidance.

An older long time mill worker with his small dog Fifi came to us after his $100,000 lottery winnings. His only request was a daily serving of fresh liver cooked with plenty of garlic for Fifi who had grown accustomed to this small luxury. His tales of the miraculous disappearance of the winnings were of great interest and very educational for our young mill workers.

Another young man, an East Coast Canadian ex-USA Marine, was hired as cook. After a fishcake breakfast our crew announced they had enough of his cooking. He requested a transfer to the mill yard. The next day he was back in the office declaring he could not work for a woman. Lynn handled our big beams with ease but the art of canter levering was not his so off he went.

Some twenty-five years later after our sawmill period there was a knock on the door. I was greeted by a confident, well dressed fellow. He introduced himself as a former student worker at our mill who had taken to heart some advice given him during his troubled time at the lake. He was now happily employed in a good position in New Jersey, USA. Others also came to tell us that their work experience in our mill was pivotal in their future direction in life.

Margo, one of our workers, went on to earn her degree in Forestry. A father came to thank us for his son's experience working at our lake mill. Another young man came to thank us for rushing him to hospital in Vancouver when he suffered acute appendicitis. No 911 then, only primitive roads and little communication.

In the early 1980s there was a serious downturn in the economy of British Columbia. The sale of recreational property declined as did the local sale of lumber. Our recreation community on the lake had expanded to where the buzzing of mill saws was not compatible with the peace and quiet desired by lot owners. It was decided under these conditions to close our lumber operation. Bruce and Lynn looked into establishing a sawmill at the former Evan's mill site on the outskirts of Pemberton.

The Canadian Federal Business Development Bank was left holding the bag as the saying goes when earlier attempts failed to revive the Pemberton Industrial Park as it was then known. The bank was keen on finding a buyer for the land and ex-mill building. It was a match made in heaven for Bruce and Lynn who wanted to continue Bruce's dream of making sawdust. They struck a deal with the bank on terms they could afford. Before long they had their own mill in operation capable of producing lumber in sufficient quantity for the export market. Brokers were ordering Pemberton lumber destined for Europe and Australia.

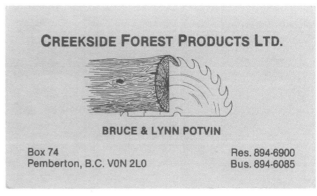

Top left photo: Bruce, Lynn and daughter Renee celebrating purchase of mill property in Pemberton, 1980s. **Centre left photo:** Newly acquired mill buildings. **Bottom photo:** Patrick loader with Renee and Kevin on board. **Centre right photo:** Lynn and Bruce's sister Heather on joining the new mill operation.

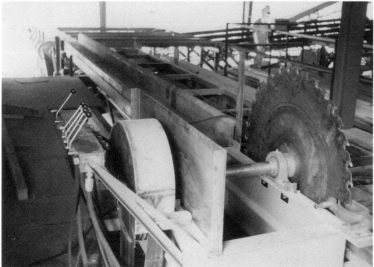

Top photo: Bruce loading a log on carriage.
Centre left photo: Head rig. **Bottom photo:**
Rollers to trim saw. Renee and Kevin. **Centre
right photo**: Finished lumber ready to be
graded and strapped.

How does all this happen? Is it just good fortune, a born skill or just hard work? Having developed the little mill at the lake whetted the appetite for a much larger mill operation. And so it was Bruce and Lynn accomplished just that.

All went well, but there was an ongoing struggle for an adequate supply of logs to keep the mill operating. Then the unexpected happened. Bruce, while inspecting a stuck hydraulic cylinder suffered a head injury of serious proportions. The mill operation closed until Bruce could resume work if that were to be possible. Worker's Compensation came into play but that did not meet business expenses while the mill was idle. Some months later Bruce was back at work. While not financially involved we offered help with additional phase funding provided by the Provincial government in the form of a loan, so as to continue employment for Bruce's loyal long term mill workers.

Again all went well until a mysterious fire broke out on the mill grounds. This was too much of a blow to overcome. The mill was closed. The Provincial Government pressed for the sale of mill assets to repay monies advanced. At this point our company was invited to oversee the dismantling of the mill. As we sold the assets creditors' bills were satisfied.

Our Lillooet Lake HJ Developments Ltd company then looked into subdividing the mill acreage into industrial sites. The Potvin entrepreneurial spirit was being put to the test. This was a risky gamble. It made sense that the growing town of Pemberton would need such a development in the future. But now? This property had already caused big time stress and major financial problems for previous owners. Would Pemberton small business owners make the gamble and move to an area on the edge of town?

The Village of Pemberton was supportive and ready to go ahead and grant the necessary approvals. The Health Department's requirements presented major challenges as to sewage disposal and source of water. The Mount Currie Native band assisted us with our water supply problem, when the Health Authority was presented with a favourable report from the laboratory the objections of the Village council were overcome.

Then came sewage disposal, a state of the art Czech Republic central treatment plant. For fire protection, a well water motor pump driven into a 40,000 gallon storage tank. Finally approval of a thirteen lot Industrial Park Development was granted.

Entrance to Pemberton Business Park.

Present day old mill building, it has now been converted to house several small businesses. CRC concrete plant is located on the adjacent site. The mill building has provided a home for many past endeavours, Evan's mill, Bruce and Lynn Potvin mill, movie site and now home to many small businesses.

Whistler Welding Company, Sandy Ryan and partner moved their plant from Whistler to the Pemberton Park to become one of the original occupants.

CHAPTER 3: CABINS ON THE LAKE

Looking along the lake one sees many beautiful cabins. It has not always been that way. Back in 1958 the thought of a cabin on the lake was very much on our minds but out of reach due to the logistics involved. It was a dream for a future date for the entrepreneurial drive to take hold.

There was no road from Vancouver, only the train to Pemberton and an expedition in a 4 wheel drive vehicle to reach the lake. In 1961 when we undertook to build, unable to hold back our entrepreneurial spirit any longer, many questioned our sanity. Four box cars were shipped to a rail siding in Mount Currie containing all the pre-cut material for a 1500 square foot cabin. With a small trailer, a new 4 wheel drive Jeep and a shortage of cash I alone had the task of hauling all this material down the lake. It was a most strenuous undertaking and one I would never be able to duplicate.

Over a period of two weeks, making three trips on most days, materials were hauled, stored and covered for the day we could find a carpenter who would brave the undertaking. The 100 sacks of cement and the asphalt roofing materials nearly did me in. The Jeep, stripped down to the driver's seat only was filled with cement bags. To steady the load a bag was placed on each end of the front bumper. The roof beams, twice the length of the trailer, dragged along the road. To prevent scarring protective plywood was nailed at the end of each beam.

When all was done it was back to the city, shirt and tie on then to the office as if this challenging undertaking had not taken place. After considerable searching a hardy carpenter and helper were found willing to rough it while constructing our dream home. This was in 1961 and now out of money, the window openings were boarded up with plywood. It was not until the following year we could afford the windows.

In 1973, sites were sold to families with an eye towards the future. No immediate building took place due to the hardships involved. In 1977, the Land Use Contract came into being. The much awaited road to Vancouver was now under construction. The tower access road down the lake was improved. All of these advancements made it possible for more site owners to consider building their dream cabins.

We at Heather Jean Properties expanded our mill operation at the lake to include the manufacture of tongue and groove logs for cabin construction. This proved so popular several cabins were built using our "Lou Logs," which facilitated assembly. With on-site lumber available cabins were being built by new owners handy with hammer and saw. Our company erected 16 or more cabins during this period.

The creation of this development has brought pleasure to many, financial gain to some, and provided employment and business for Pemberton people. This did not happen without a lot of hard work, dedication and addressing the frustrations that arise with any enterprise. The greatest satisfaction is having been able to share with others the beautiful setting of Lillooet Lake. This chapter tells the stories of a few cabins and their owners, however there are many more to admire; some of the stories are written by the owners themselves.

KURT AND MARLENE POETZSCHKE

We had been looking for a recreational property for several years, when we noticed an ad in the Vancouver Sun at the beginning of March 1974. We had never heard of Lillooet Lake before and assumed it was somewhere near Lillooet. However, after talking to Carol we were assured that it is much closer to Vancouver, so we took the trip up there to take a look. It was the 15th of March and Whistler was hit with a major snowstorm. We got stuck in a deep snowdrift on Suicide Hill close to Pemberton and had to be towed out. We figured that was no weekend to look at property. So we stayed at the Pemberton Hotel overnight with plans to return to Vancouver in the morning. We talked to Louis on the phone to let him know we were unable to see the property in all that snow, and Louis said "what snow?" Apparently there was no snow at the lake, so he came to meet us in Mt. Currie and we followed him down that steep hill to the lake. Luckily that scary hill is no more.

We took one look at the available lots and knew right away which one we wanted. That was the beginning of more than 39 years of beautiful memories at Lillooet Lake. However, it also was a lot of hard work clearing the lot of logs and brush while we lived in a tent. In those days there was a lot of wildlife around. I was literally watched by a big black bear when I was digging holes for the cabin footings. We also had a couple of grouse living on our property and occasionally we would see a bobcat. There were mink running along the shore and otters playing in front of our lot.

Water for washing was hauled up from the lake and we brought big drums of drinking water from Vancouver. By spring of 1977 we had enough of a clearing to start building our log cabin and by fall we had the roof on and windows and doors in. The cabin started to look pretty good. After that I had several projects every year to get the place to where it is now.

Our two children Lisa and Brian have had lots of good times at the lake swimming, boating, and fishing. On land there were Easter egg hunts, building tree forts and hiking up Joffre. Now there are grandchildren who will hopefully appreciate our cabin as much as we did. Things are getting easier every year with year round running water, road improvements, and our new solar system.

Visitors to our place always admire the postcard view of the mountains from our lot and the word paradise has been mentioned many times. Well we think it is, and hopefully we can enjoy it for a few more years.

The first abode in 1975

Brian having fun

The Log Cabin

Brian with Easter eggs

Kurt & Marlene

Brian & Lisa

Kurt & his Dolly

Kurt with his mother Luise & his daughter Lisa on Louis & Carol's houseboat

Kurt and Marlene Poetzcheke.

This corner site is Lot 1 in Lillooet Lake Estates owned and developed by David Boyle. The scenic location, attractive dwelling dock and landscaping enjoys a one of a kind view of the lake and mountains.

SHARON AND LORNE CRAIG

I am proud to have been a Director of Lillooet Lake Estates, and in that process humbly learned a lot about building a community from the ground up. Even with all the ups and downs of politics at the micro-community level, there is a real satisfaction in seeing people come together to create a resilient 'village' in the midst of a beautiful wilderness. It gives us a genuine appreciation of the pioneering spirit that built this country. We have raised our family and built a home here over the last 17 years. Our son has caught, cleaned and cooked his own fish, he can chop wood, drive a nail and ski powder. Lillooet Lake really has been the backdrop to the best times of our lives.

Winter scene of Craig Cabin.

Lorne and Sharon Craig.

HORST JOOST

Horst was one of the early owners of property in Lillooet Lake Estates. From Bavaria, part of Germany, Horst came with an inborn love of the forest, trees and the art of working with wood. He purchased a post and beam deck already erected by HJ Developments on his chosen piece of forest high on the hill overlooking the lake and mountains. Horst applied his skills to a Bavarian style dwelling with matching stonework.

After retirement Horst moved to live permanently at the lake. Retirement did not mean idleness; his wood, stone and metal works continue to grace his property. Even with his ongoing projects Horst finds time to contribute to the lake community. He walks daily as an informal watchman and gathers wood debris on adjoining Crown Land so as to minimize the fire hazard in the surrounding area. His daughter and grandchild often visit from the city to enjoy his wooded retreat. Below are photos of Horst's work.

Horst's Cabin.

Horst's fireplace.

Horst's Gazebo

GARY AND JILL YOUNG

In 1986 the Young family from North Vancouver joined our growing community of lake enthusiasts. Lot-40 cabin was already in place on the lake shore when it was spotted by the Youngs during a camping trip to Strawberry Point. With a background of Ontario lake and cottage life the cabin fit their dreams and they made it their own.

Boats and water sports were a major interest so much so that Jay, the oldest boy was doing a Polar Bear water ski on New Year's Day. The many wonderful memories of the family growing up adventuring at the lake are family treasures ready to be passed on to the next generation.

In recent years the Lot-40 summer home and grounds have enjoyed a handsome remodelling to become their principal home as Gary and Jill semi-retire from their busy business lives to spend more time at Lillooet Lake.

Gary & Jill

Gary and Jill.

Lake shore Lot-40 cabin site.

LIZ AND EDUARD KLASSEN

The evolution of ownership of this site and the dwelling Ed and Liz constructed presents an interesting story. In year 1977 Papa Klassen approached us to purchase a lakeside site. Papa, Ed and brother Eric pooled their resources and purchased Lot-10. It was not long after brother Eric and wife Judy were able to purchase their own lake shore site. Ed, Liz and children Brenda and Randy camped on their property for a number of years. Every summer the extended Klassen family of Papa, Mama, brothers, sister and the third generation enjoyed their passion for water skiing.

During year 1994 Ed and Liz started construction on their dream cabin not realizing this would become their principal home. Lumber from the Heather Jean sawmill at the lake was used in their cabin. Later Dr. Bowie in Gate 1 generously parted with several large Heather Jean cut beams left over after construction of the Bowie Cabin. These beams are featured overhead in Ed and Liz's living room. If it had not been for this fortunate source of supply the beams may have been more modest in size, as these large beams were no longer being produced.

In the year 2001 Ed and Liz moved to the lake. Ed has now been employed by Heather Jean for over 13 years. The photo shown illustrates the quality workmanship Ed and Liz devoted to the construction of their home. Every summer Liz's wild flower garden spills a cascade of colour from their deck to the water's edge to be much enjoyed by boaters passing by.

Ed and Liz Klassen Cabin, Lot-10.

Ed and Liz Klassen.

PAUL AND KERRIE PALMER

We first discovered Strawberry Point, which is still one of my favourite camp sites anywhere. Not long after, Kerrie and I were enjoying a Sunday morning in the city, having brunch, sipping coffee and reading the paper, when Kerrie read out an ad from the classified section: "A small cabin on half acre lot, 45 minutes from Whistler, at Lillooet Lake Estates" for a price that seemed very reasonable for the area. Brunch ended, and we went for a drive, however, about three hours later when we learned of the unique shared ownership, that "reasonable price" was now unachievable due to the difficulty in obtaining a mortgage. But we came away with a new plan. Lots above the road were going for between twenty and thirty thousand dollars. We closed the deal on our little piece of paradise in the fall of 1999.

In tents, VW vans, and RVs we spent the days brushing and clearing, and the nights drawing, dreaming, sketching, and scheming. In the spring of 2002 we moved from the city to Pemberton, into a three bedroom townhouse. So now we had a "build it yourselfer" and a "fix it up yourselfer". Good thing my "day job" was at night. Slowly but surely we plugged along, my wife working days while working on her master's degree at night, and me working nights while building during the day. SLOW by the way stands for A LOT of work.

In the fall of 2009 we sold our townhouse and moved into our 300 square foot cabin, three years later we finally call the house a home. Being full timers in the boondocks has its share of challenges, but these are more than offset by the rewards. A million dollar sunset, 365 sunsets a year, do the math!

Kerrie now works as a clinical counsellor in Mt. Currie, Pemberton and Whistler, and I continue to plug away on the finishing touches on the house, as well as landscaping, including a deck and steps for the wood fired hot tub. I still spend a couple of nights a week crafting cocktails and mixing martinis in Whistler as ski season passes aren't cheap. At the same time I keep busy working on the Lillooet Lake Estates water system and other parts of our public works.

We love life at Lillooet Lake, it may not be for everyone, but I think that's the point. We enjoy the peace and tranquillity, while still being part of a small, sustainable, and co-operative community.

Paul and Kerrie Palmer Cabin.   Paul and Kerrie Palmer.

Michelle designed her cabin with her three children, their nine cousins and numerous friends in mind. Many great family gatherings have ensued and memories made, all confirming her foresight and planning skills. A large solar array provides light to ensure games can be played and puzzles completed.

Michelle St. Pierre with sand and water loving family dog, Carmela on lakefront.

VINCE AND LOUISE HOLMES

In 1979, we at HJ Developments built a cabin on site 162 to display our new tongue and groove construction. Vince and Louise answered our small classified ad in the Vancouver Sun and came looking. The perfect setting of sunshine, lake and mountains helped along with the scent of fresh cut cedar sealed the deal on the spot.

The Vince and Louise team of handyman and artistic skill set to work and was soon hosting family and friends for weekend gatherings at the Holmestead. Good times were also shared cruising the lake on the Potvin houseboat the Carolou. When the time came to sell the Holmestead, the Holmes said the happy days spent at the lake were some of the best of their lives. This is a true reward for an entrepreneur.

The Holmestead has had several owners since the early days, they too have made their mark on this little cabin. It is not unreasonable to say the happy atmosphere of the Holmestead lingers on after all these years.

The Holmes cabin of years gone by.

Louise and Vince Holmes.

DOUG AND SANDY REMPEL

Energy-efficiency has been a business career as well as a passion of mine for over 30 years. Sandy and I have been working in the heating and ventilation industry helping people build super-efficient homes. This is what we have done with our place at Lillooet Lake. My other involvements in energy efficiency off the grid include appearing on radio talk shows, teaching workshops at schools, and appearing on HGTV. To back track a bit, I'm a bit of an energy nut. I documented this process in a blog which I call Going Off the Grid.

The first 6km portion of the Lillooet Lake lake shore sites are 600 feet in elevation and facing south. The 7,000 foot mountains across the lake are high enough to provide full winter solar gain on the south windows right up until December 21 when the sun angles are lowest. This portion of the lake runs east-west; we get a very early sunrise and a very late sunset.

We love Lillooet Lake's close proximity to Vancouver, the mild winter and hot summer weather. The fishing, hiking, emerald waters, and majestic mountains which surround us is an invitation for kayaking and boating. We very much appreciate the community of people in this development, Lillooet Lake Estates and Heather Jean Properties. We have made many new friends we truly consider to be rare jewels which we are fortunate to have discovered.

Rempel Cabin.

Sandy and Doug Rempel.

PAUL AND AYA ST. PIERRE

Years ago when I was a young boy my father would take me fishing to what is known as the Narrows where Lillooet Lake drains into the smaller lake below and the fish are plentiful. To get there was only for the brave as there was no road, only the hydro tower access trails joined together by those in the logging industry. The steep hill past Joffre Creek with tumbling rocks added to the excitement.

Years later my mother Carol Potvin and her husband Louis developed building sites on Lillooet Lake. I am proud to say my wife Aya and I have a site and cabin in this development. This has brought us and our children Marc and Mireille much pleasure over the years.

What was once an isolated place to go and fish with solitude is now being shared by many, however, enough of the magic that I enjoyed as a young boy remains. The beautiful surroundings and changes with the seasons is a scenic wonder we never tire of viewing.

Paul and Aya's cabin.   Aya and Paul St. Pierre.

ALLEN AND CONNIE CLEAVER

One day two motorcyclists, in full gear, arrived at the lake to enquire about property. My first reaction was, "Oh No", what do we have here Hells Angels? It took tough people to descend the steep hills of those days, the road could hardly be called one and it dropped straight to the lake. To my surprise the helmets came off to reveal regular people, not at all what I expected. Al was the Surrey Fire Chief and Connie was a mother and school teacher/librarian.

In no time Al and Connie chose the site of their liking. Our Heather Jean mill was across the road and again in no time Al had erected their cabin "THE BARN". Al and my son Bruce established a bond that had Bruce pushing the crew to provide custom cut lumber for the BARN construction. This was during 1979/80.

Connie and Al spent many happy days at the BARN often hosting get togethers for neighbours at the lake. Al served as President of the Lot Owners group during the formative years offering firefighting training and setting workable policies that remain in place today.

The BARN after many years of enjoyment by the Cleaver family was sold to new owners who valued the quality workmanship and enjoyed skiing in nearby Whistler. Connie has passed away and is missed by all. Al resides in Surrey where for some time he hosted a cable television show for seniors often featuring the history of the Lower Mainland and our area.

The BARN as it looks today.

ROBIE AND JANET THORN

Robie is an accounting professional recently retired from his own practice which had offices in Whistler and Squamish. There he provided his clients with accounting and tax services. Prior to that Robie spent a number of years in corporate financing with the Federal Business Development Bank, the Bank of British Columbia, and the North Shore Credit Union, eventually transferring to Whistler where he managed the Whistler Branch. Coincidently, during his time with the Federal Business Development Bank he was involved in the initial financing of a land development company at Lillooet Lake owned by Louis Potvin. Small world.

During his years as a Whistler resident Robie was very active in the community serving as co-President of the Whistler Community Services Society, President of the Rotary Club of Whistler, and Director of the Whistler Chamber of Commerce. He also found time to volunteer as a gate judge for a number of World Cup downhill skiing events and the 2010 winter Olympics.

Robie joined the Board of Lillooet Lake Estates Ltd. in 2002 and served as Treasurer for a number of years, becoming President in 2010. His focus is the completion of numerous infrastructure projects and moving forward to making Lillooet Lake Estates a viable year round living community for full time residents, and a desired vacation place for part time residents.

Robie Thorn and his wife Janet have chosen to live full time at the lake creating an outstanding combination of cabin and surrounding landscaping. Lots of work but beautiful to view.

The cabin at Lillooet Lake Estates has been our vacation home since June 1993. Ralph and I decided to venture out within a few hours of Vancouver looking for a rustic place in the woods to call our own. The idea of a place we could drive to any weekend to get away from the busy city life was our dream.

Lillooet Lake provided us with everything we were looking for including tall snow-capped mountains so characteristic of the west coast, the natural wonder of the evergreen forest, and the seasonal changing green colour of the lake water. The cabin itself was a pleasant surprise built from "Lou logs" milled at Lillooet Lake, a traditional wood stove for heat, and the ambience of oil lanterns and candles at night.

Getting away from the city to Lillooet Lake makes us feel more alive and energized but still allows us time for peaceful reflection and solitude. There are projects to tinker with keeping our minds active while at the same time being laid back and enjoying the outdoors. The fresh air draws us outside along with fun activities on the lake such as fishing, water-skiing, hiking, and ATV riding. Our children have found simpler enjoyment in playing games such as hide-and-seek, tag, board games and cards. Our family dog "Susie", who has passed away, would jump out of her slumber in the vehicle once the tires touched the gravel road leading to the cabin, knowing soon she would be at her favourite place.

Many of our friends and family have come to the lake over the years commenting "this is a wonderful piece of paradise," to which we must agree and hope in the years ahead our children and grandchildren will keep coming to enjoy Lillooet Lake as much as we have.

Ralph and Karen Cabin, Lot-25.

Karen and Ralph.

CAROL AND LOUIS POTVIN

The Potvins have lived full time at the lake since 1965, time to experience many changes; the birth of Heather Jean Estates Ltd., Lillooet Lake Estates Ltd. and changes to Heather Jean Properties Ltd. We also think of more historical times. We think of the others who have made this lake and river corridor their home or arrived to explore and search for elusive riches.

Today, as before, First Nations continue in their historical communities actively using their traditional lands. One hundred and fifty years ago the lake hosted early gold rush prospectors who built trails along the lake shore and sailed sternwheelers up the Lillooet, Anderson and Seton lakes. Now present day prospectors comb our mountains and streams for signs of valuable metals. Others come to harness electric power from our rivers. Logging companies have come, gone and are now returning.

Lot-50D cabin was built on the abandoned Fleetwood Logging site of the 1940s and 1950's. The company logged our lake shore and the timber across the lake with tugs and log booms, loading at the head of the lake where now the only visible signs of their presence are the abandoned pilings at the mouth of the Birkenhead River. It is said there is a sunken tug not far off the Lot-50D dock, the victim of a sudden violent wind storm.

Our cabin too has seen many changes since it was first built in the sixties. As our permanent home, it has continued to serve as office/ headquarters for the various enterprises that have kept Louis and family busy over the years. A mink ranch, the birth of Heather Jean Estates Ltd., sawmill, planer mill, radio station, industrial park, even a bit of logging have changed Lot-50D. Our cabin has served as bunk house, cook house, dining hall, office, emergency medical centre, and communication centre. It has been home and home away from home for many fine young people, our children, twelve grandchildren, and friends.

Photo 1: Carolou at small swimming beach down the lake.

Photo 2: Family dog Daisy, Carol and Louis relaxing aboard the Carolou.

Photo 3: Potvin home and office.

Photo 4: Captain Louis.

Photo 5: Office garden.

Photo 6: Garden and lake from the Potvin office.

Photo 7: Suzanne St. Pierre tying up the Carolou

Photo 1: Lake with beach and breakwater.
Photo 2: Lake reflections; lake extends another 10 miles around point of view.
Photo 3: Winter shore line.
Photo 4: Winter scene; Potvin home and office.
Photo 5: Willow tree with swings on lakeshore.
Photo 6: Moonlight on the lake.
Photo 7: Family companion "Daisy" cooling off before sailing.

CHAPTER 4: ENJOYING THE LAKE

What is it that has attracted our neighbours to Lillooet Lake? Namely the development we gave birth to on DL-4901 – 3/4 mile lake frontage. Nature lovers are content being near water with scenic mountains around, some burning the generous wood supply at their door. Then there is boating of all sorts; fishing and hiking too. Those who have come and gone enjoyed a financial gain as well as the pleasure of ownership.

Lillooet Lake's close proximity to Vancouver is a main attraction, a wilderness reached without exhausting travel. Organized activities are not far away; Whistler skiing and Pemberton golfing and horseback riding. There is an airport in Pemberton for small planes and trails in all directions for hikers, bikers and horseback riding.

In this chapter we have illustrated many of the pleasurable things Lot Owners have done. In our case we had a dream of a boat on Lillooet Lake. This dream came true with the houseboat Carolou sailing the lake for almost 20 years. It has been a treasure without measure for family and friends, and frequently a help in our business. Drifting down the lake aboard the Carolou we enjoyed the feeling we were truly part of nature's world.

When we purchased property on Lillooet Lake in 1958 we were keen on being weekend gardeners. Bob Taylor the agent through which we purchased our property told us the lake area was ideal for gardening and growing fruit trees. It had a warmer climate that allowed early frost free planting with its southern exposure. It was drier than coastal areas being located in the divide between a coastal climate and the warmer interior. His words served us well as we found this to be the case.

Every year Carol had a vegetable garden. I planted fruit trees year after year. Our crops were so plentiful we would load up the car and offer our produce free of charge. It is only in recent years we have had bear problems and the destruction of some of our trees. A vegetable garden was not enough for Carol, however, and the property was adorned with flower beds.

Photo 1: Eastern Redbud tree. Beautiful flowers every spring. **Photo 2:** Dark purple Lilacs bordering the Raspberry patch. **Photo 3:** Forsythia, tulips and blossoming plum tree. **Photo 4:** Dogwood tree, replanted from wild growth, about 12 inches in height. It does well beside the Rhododendrons. After 20 years it is now 30 ft. tall. **Photo 5:** A flower border, staked tomatoes, apple trees and the lake. **Photo 6:** Carol with "Mammoth" sunflowers reaching for the sky.

Our flowers at the lake flourish in spite of sparse sandy, rocky soil. However, we do talk to them and they do their best in return.

Photo 1: Hydrangea.
Photo 2: Cactus.
Photo 3: Carpet Roses.
Photo 4: Amaranth.
Photo 5: Yellow Roses (bloom yearly, sent by the Henrys upon my son Bruce passing).
Photo 6: Begonia in pot.

Photo 1: Liz Klassen at the wheel towing Ross Marino enjoying his new experience. **Photo 2:** Family group heading off for a trip on the lake, Suzanne St. Pierre, Carol pushing off. Alex and Ross Marino and Kevin Potvin eager to go. **Photo 3:** Michelle St. Pierre, Carol's daughter, soaking up the lake sun. **Photo 4:** Louis Potvin about to take off to the stream across the lake. **Photo 5:** Louis with sailboat in pre-Carolou days. When anchored out gathering rain water we sometimes found Dolly Varden fish swimming in the bottom of the hull, having jumped out of the lake and landed by accident into the boat. How much easier can it be for dinner? **Photo 6:** Potvin family group tied up at a sandy beach down the lake. This beach was the late Dan Moon's favourite spot. We all knew it as Moon Beach. Dan, a Lot Owner, was a Court Judge who moved to the city. Dan's dog Daisy became the Potvin's special companion spending her final days at Heather Jean Properties at the lake.

What is the strong attraction our family and other families feel for Lillooet Lake? What kind of spell has this 16 mile body of water, essentially a widening of the Lillooet River making its way to the ocean, cast upon us? We love the beauty, the feeling of solitude, we feel strong in the confirmation that we are part of the real world, nature's world. At the lake it is always exciting to be busy, to be quiet, to be creative, to be challenged, often it is being ourselves. Most of all it is where all of us have fun, from grandparents to toddlers.

Photo 1: Rose Moon a Lot Owner catching the wind. **Photo 2:** Suzanne St. Pierre drifting along (Carol's daughter). **Photo 3:** Marc St. Pierre, grandson and friend exchanging ideas on the water (Paul St. Pierre's son). **Photo 4:** Marc St. Pierre and Michael Vidler (Suzanne St. Pierre's son), grandchildren travelling the lake on their self-made raft. **Photo 5:** Neighbours sailing by. **Photo 6:** Marc St. Pierre heading in to the dock. **Photo 7:** Paul St. Pierre, Carol's son, enjoying his Kayak; the Carolou in the background.

ENJOYING THE PEMBERTON VALLEY

The Pemberton airport is only a 30 minute drive from the lake. Some owners of sites fly in on occasion. Others have enjoyed a flight in a glider, or just come and view the aircraft taking off and landing. Some owners of sites fly in on occasion, others have enjoyed a glider flight from the airport, or just come and view the aircraft taking off and landing.

Photo 1: The Canadian Forces Snowbirds lined up at the Pemberton Airport ready to delight the many onlookers. **Photo 2:** Snowbirds against steep and rugged Mount Currie. This was to be a one time performance as the mountainous area was considered too risky for a repeat performance. **Photo 3:** Looking up the Lillooet River from the head of Lillooet Lake. **Photo 4:** Flying over the Village of Pemberton. **Photo 5:** Looking up the Valley past Mount Currie; Green River on the left and the Lillooet River on the right. **Photo 6:** Looking down on Lillooet Lake. The Hydro Line and Road at the bottom of the photo is DL-4901 where our development is located.

On New Year's Day 2013 a spontaneous Polar Bear Swim was conceived and implemented in minutes on the beach in front of the Marino cabin. A driftwood campfire was quickly built to warm chilly bodies emerging from the waters of the lake.

Photo 1: Paul St. Pierre and family dog Kona in viewing position. At the water's edge Ross Marino. Don MacDonald, Gillian Marino and friend Nathaniel from Boston. **Photo 2:** The Marinos: Alexander, Michelle, Gillian and Nathaniel sharing their cold water thoughts. **Photo 3:** Into the lake! Marc St. Pierre, Gillian and Nathaniel. **Photo 4:** Out of the lake Nathaniel and Marc. **Photo 5:** Ross heading for the warmth of the campfire. **Photo 6:** Gillian and Nathaniel again. **Photo 7:** Brave swimmers taking a bow: Don MacDonald, Ross Marino, Gillian Marino, Nathaniel and Marc St. Pierre. **Photo 8:** Polar Bear swimmers posing in front of Michelle St. Pierre cabin.

In 1958 when we first spent weekends and holidays at our Lillooet Lake retreat fishing was one of the main attractions. We could troll for a couple of hours and were sure of catching a fish or two. Dolly Varden mostly, and cutthroat at the right time of year. My son Bruce, an enthusiastic young fisherman, would bring a friend from school for the weekend experience.

Our boat with an 18 HP outboard motor allowed the boys in a very short time to cover several creeks that entered the lake. Bruce kept a log of fish they caught, with the time, date and location. Every time the boys went fishing we were assured of a catch of 7 or more fish. The small creeks were good for 2 fish at most then it was time to move to the mouth of another creek. Lizzie Creek was good for 3 to 4 fish.

There were times other species the same in size appeared in quantity with a frenzy to bite the lure, never to be seen again. At that time I was so interested in these fishing events that I developed a contact in the Provincial Ministry with whom I discussed our experiences. It was a two way street, we learned and they confirmed.

The Narrows where the lake drains into a lower smaller lake was a popular place to fish. In the early spring when the salmon fry were running it was no problem to catch your limit in a very short time. Large size Dolly Varden would gobble up so many fry that when we unfastened the hook from their mouths fry were hanging out of their gills. In our first book "LOUIS PLACE" there is a photo of one afternoon's catch. This exciting fishing experience could be repeated several times during the season.

Photo 1: Louis and Carol's daughter Michelle fishing at Ure Creek (Boulder Creek).

Photo 2: Michael Vidler, grandson, with fish ready for the pan.

Photo 3: Rosemary Morgan, granddaughter with grandpa hauling in a Dolly.

Photo 4: Marc St. Pierre with his first catch.

Photo 5: Grandpa Lou on the Carolou with fish and fork in hand ready for the frying pan.

Photo 6: Douglas Morgan, grandson, happy with his catch.

Photo 7: Granddaughter Renee casting at Lizzie Creek.

Kurt Poetzschke Lot Owner is a master of Lillooet Lake fishing. Kurt quietly goes about his favourite sport, the results shown on the enclosed photos. Fishing has been one of the big attractions for Lot Owners.

In addition to the resident fish in the lake there are ocean runs like Coho, Spring and Sockeye passing through. There were Steelhead in the early years but scarce today. First Native residents have reported their elders many years ago observing sturgeon at the head of the lake. Salmon spawn in the Birkenhead and Lillooet Rivers and their tributaries. Seals are sometimes spotted in the lake having followed the Salmon migration from the salt waters of the coast.

Photo 1: Cutthroat trout. **Photo 2:** Kurt Poetzschke's son Brian learning how to fish. **Photo 3:** Dolly Varden's revenge. **Photo 4:** An afternoon catch for Kurt. **Photo 5:** Renee at her young age actually hooked on to a big one. **Photo 6:** Kurt with another afternoon catch. **Photo 7:** Son Brian is a quick learner.

Exploration, adventure, and pursuits of nature's knowledge are all around us – we have only to embrace the opportunities. In the mountains above our lake communities there is a most beautiful little lake. For the greater part of the year it is hidden under the snow and ice of the higher elevation and colder temperature. From Lillooet Lake in the summer we can study the terrain, the configuration of the valleys and streams running down the mountainside into our larger lake. It is the path of water that supplies the in-ground spring for local water systems. One day we made a trip by helicopter from our former mill yard to this lovely little emerald coloured lake.

Photo 1: At the emerald coloured alpine lake, Michelle Marino, Jacqueline St. Pierre, Alexander and Gillian Marino. **Photo 2:** Paraglider high over the mountains. **Photo 3:** To the left the pilot and I are resting. In the centre is Alexander Marino, cousin Jacqueline St. Pierre and Ross Marino. **Photo 4:** Several high rocky areas along the lake are home to First Nation's pictographs, now unfortunately fading away from the ravages of weather over time. This one in the photo depicts a fish, perhaps a salmon, as the salmon runs are a valuable food source. **Photo 5:** Gillian Marino and Nathaniel from Boston enjoying the shelter built by a previous camper at Strawberry Beach up lake from our property.

PEMBERTON DRAGON BOAT TEAM ON LILLOOET LAKE

The CBC television crew were here to film the Pemberton Dragon Boat teams from the Carolou. It was a beautiful day in May year 2002. The filming was for the TV series "On the Road Again".

Now in year 2013 the Laoyom Eagles have just completed their 15th straight championship win at the Rio Tinto Alcan Dragon Boat Festival in Vancouver. Eight of the Eagle Paddlers represented Canada at the World Championships in Hungary in the summer of 2013. The Dragon Paddlers are high school students from Mount Currie, Pemberton and surrounding areas, cheered and supported by the residents of the community. Liam Fisher and George Henry, grandson of Shirley and George Henry, are seated in front of the steersman in the aluminium canoe.

WINTER FUN AT THE LAKE

The summer months are not the only time one can enjoy Lillooet Lake. While we do not have a frozen lake to skate on we do have snow. Here is a snow filled December day when the grandchildren and their friends are having fun at the Potvin's, sliding down the slope to the beach. This was a happy and bonding day for all. Fun is where you make it.

Photo 1: Sliding down in front of Louis' old mink shed. In the toboggan is Mireille and father Paul St. Pierre. To their left is Kristen Sullivan and Mireille at another time. **Photo 2 & 5:** Mireille St. Pierre swinging under the Willow tree and sliding down the slope. **Photo 3:** Marc and sister Mireille of the St. Pierre family **Photo 4:** Even the big kids got into the fun. Kevin Potvin and sister Renee MacDonald with cousin Rosemary Morgan, Louis' grandchildren.

LIVING IN THE MOUNTAINS

The province of British Columbia is made up of mountains, rivers, streams, and valleys. This beauty has its hazards as do the more open spaces in Canada. Many valley floors were covered with water in years gone by. These areas are where we find our towns and cities being the only flat land available. Nature's hand is never static, the mountains erode, their contents taken down by streams, rivers and lakes into the ocean. The Lillooet Lake area is no different from other areas.

The Sea to Sky highway admired by many throughout the world was constructed through an area of wash outs, rock slides and hazardous crossings. Proper planning and remedial work brought us this beautiful highway we all enjoy today. It was not always so. When Carol and I first went on air, Mountain FM Radio was the only guide as to whether the road was open or closed.

Lillooet Lake is an extension of the Pemberton Valley commencing from the Lillooet glacier. The village of Pemberton some years ago suffered from water entering the elementary school grounds. This was remedied by restoring the creek channel emptying into One Mile Lake. More recently the Pemberton area was placed on an evacuation notice due to a gigantic slide at Meager Creek. This is at the head of the valley, inland of the coastal range located many miles upstream from the farms and village. The hazard diminished and things went back to normal with a watchful eye on the Meager Creek area.

The Lillooet Lake area is not immune to torrents of water and debris flows. This was taken into account when the area was under approval for recreational and residential sites. Protection corridors were established along the creek channel. An engineer advised the creek channel was to be kept unobstructed, including bridge crossings. During the earlier years there was remedial work done on the creek channel. Mountains are continually changing and this is what takes place above our development. At higher elevations there is crumbling causing debris flows that need to be contained. Now in 2013 new engineering studies are underway that will direct additional improvements to protect our enjoyment of the lake.

CHAPTER 5: ANIMAL LIFE: OBSERVATIONS AND ENCOUNTERS

After purchasing our lake frontage on Lillooet Lake every possible weekend was spent travelling by PGE train to Pemberton, then on to the lake to explore our new summer get away. We had our small Shasta Trailer shipped in ready for our arrival on these late nights. The trip down the road in the dark nearly always provided the sight of an animal or two. Bears, Lynx, Coyote, Skunk, Porcupine, Deer, Wolverine, Racoons – the works – one time even a Moose ran by.

Bears are interesting to see but not around your premises or your fruit trees as they can be very destructive. Included is a collage of bear photos taken before the fruit trees were nearly destroyed. In early summer older males sometimes attack the young cubs. Mother and cubs usually make a run for it when a mature male enters their feeding area. Bears like clover and we have clover in our lawns so we see these visitors grazing like cattle in our backyard.

Racoons live by our small creek. Grapes are one of their favourite meals. At night we hear them run across our roof to the grape arbor. Once we saw a raccoon steal a kitten from the cat bed in the carport. Deer also like to visit in the spring for a feast of opening tulip buds.

The mountain side is well stocked with what we call a pack rat, known as a mountain rat in some circles. Unlike a harbour rat a pack rat has a nice coat, a furry tail and long ears, and is very clever at entering through the smallest openings. I have witnessed one deflate itself and squeeze through under a door only to pump itself up once inside – I had some 30 plastic trays in the repair shop filled overnight with freshly cut mushrooms to dry for a winter food supply. They appear to keep two nests, one in use and one other at a different location. The spare nest is frequently found with door keys, nails and screws which the rat has gathered. One pack rat kept us awake all night as we wondered where all the thump, thump was coming from. The rat was lining up all the newly picked tomatoes from the kitchen, placing these in rows at the top of the stairs, nudging them one at a time to roll to the bottom of the stairway. Now that is called planning ahead.

Our cats mostly from barn stock are fully domesticated but during the summer months like to take off for several days at a time. They return to be fed more as a ritual as they are well fed in the wild. My two cats at the moment have learned how to shake a paw. One must have much patience in training a cat as they only respond when it is in their mind to do so; not like a dog eager to please. One cat we had took off the first day of spring and returned soon as the weather was cold. This cat would appear at the door and upon entering would make a direct run to the feeding area imprinted in the cat's mind.

Mice at the lake can be a challenge even with the help of the cats if care is not taken. As fast as the mice are disposed of the mountain side brings replacements. If one leaves a box of kindling wood or a box of supplies outdoors too long, when it is taken indoors the mice come hidden inside.

We have included bird information submitted by John Tschopp, a knowledgeable birder from up the Pemberton Valley. John operated a machine shop for several years and looks after our needs from time to time. We are grateful John has shared his bird information with us as his observations of birds apply to the lake area as well.

One collage covers dogs that lived with us during their short life span. Sandy a German Sheppard was a rare find as to intelligence. It was apparent after a few months this dog was special. We lived in the city at the time and I trained Sandy myself. This dog loved the lake and chased bears away. Daisy was another remarkably intelligent dog given to us by Rose and Dan Moon. Losing Daisy was like losing a member of the family as that is what Daisy had become. Today we have no dog, a void in our lives that we can no longer fill.

John Tschopp Collection

Photo 1: John scanning the skies from the Pemberton Valley farm fields. **Photo 2:** A young Short Eared Owl. **Photo 3:** A Rufous Hummingbird. These birds are common at the lake always arriving at precisely the same time as the wild flowering currant bush blooms. **Photo 4:** The Red Breasted Sapsucker, a noisy fellow as he drills his nesting hole. **Photo 5:** A Sharp-shinned Hawk. **Photo 6:** An American Robin, always a cheery sight when they arrive in early spring.

John Tschopp Collection

Photo 1: Evening Grosbeak, one of the many colourful birds that frequent the lake. Flocks fly fast and low over our garden area, we have had to duck to avoid a collision. **Photo 2:** Black Headed Grosbeak, another seed eater with dramatic colouring. **Photo 3:** Northern Flicker. The Flickers at the lake are not shy, often drilling nest holes in our out-buildings. **Photo 4:** Black-capped Chickadee enjoying a meal of sunflower seeds. **Photo 5:** Bohemian Waxwing is always smooth and dapper, never a feather out of place. **Photo 6:** Steller's Jay, our Jays stay around most of the winter enjoying their morning breakfast hour on our deck.

John Tschopp Collection

Photo 1: Pileated Woodpecker with young. Everything about this bird is large; size 41-48 centimetres, large bright red crest, loud call and large nest holes. **Photo 2:** Osprey, a fish hawk that patrols up and down the lake. The dive for a fish may or may not be successful. Even with fish in talons an eagle may attempt a takeover as we once witnessed. The birds engaged in a spectacular aerial display all in vain; the fish was lost and fell back into the lake. **Photo 3:** Mallard ducks flocking up in the fall preparing for the flight to warmer weather in the south. **Photo 4:** Western Tanager, one of Carol's favourite birds, always arrives as the Saskatoon berries ripen. **Photo 5:** Common Loon. One day we watched Mother Loon swim by with a single chick on her back. Baby jumped off Mom, without glancing back or changing her paddling rhythm Mom swept her wing to the side, scooped up baby and placed it right back where it belonged. **Photo 6:** Crows frequent our cherry trees in early summer. Later we see them at the head of the lake when the salmon are spawning. When Carol's daughter Suzanne was a young girl she had a pet Crow. Missy the Crow learned to say "Hello Pretty Girl".

ED KLASSEN'S BIRD PHOTOS

These photos except for photo 5 were taken the spring of 2013 by Ed who has just recently been bitten by the "birding bug".

Photo 1: The Eurasian Collared dove, an import from Europe, has been spreading its territory north from the Los Angeles area. This is the first year the Doves have nested at Heather Jean Properties. **Photo 2:** Raven, a large crow like bird enjoys harvesting our cherry and apple crops. **Photo 3:** Common Merganser often nests close by. One year 12 chicks were produced. The chicks were lined up on our breakwater log for their first swimming lesson. Sadly, two or three days later when ready to swim up the lake the chicks were reduced in numbers. **Photo 4:** Sooty Grouse visits our vegetable garden during the summer to feed on zucchinis. **Photo 5:** Domestic geese; were pets of son Bruce and wife Lynn when they lived at the lake with their children Renee and Kevin. The lure of wild geese on the lake drew the barnyard geese out to visit the family connection. After visiting the wild ones they would paddle back home. One day a roaming coyote attacked one pet goose, returning the next day for the second. Lillooet Lake never lacks interest of some kind be it birds, animals, humans, or acts of nature. **Photo 6:** A flock of Canada Geese resting on Lillooet Lake before continuing north to their breeding ground.

Who is the intruder? In recent years black bears have frequently dropped by for a snack, an inevitable outcome with so many cabins in the area. In the early days of the developing community there was not much to attract the bears except for the wild berries. There was excitement when a bear would wander by. Nowadays it is hide the garbage and hope the fruit trees will be overlooked.

In year 2012 a cub was left behind and starving with no mother. The cub sought refuge under a nearby cabin. The Game Warden was notified, who arrived to transport the cub to a Langley sanctuary to be fattened up over the winter and released in the spring. The sanctuary commented this was the worst condition of a bear they had ever seen. Come summer, tagged on one ear, this cub having grown considerably over the winter arrived at the lake office window as she had done the year before. This is the bear in the photo by the garden hose. With the bear's nose pressed

against the window pane I too did the same thing. Here we were nose to nose with only a sheet of glass between us. I peered back looking deeply into the bears dark blue eyes and felt a sort of a chill and a connection with the bear. I felt as though the young bear was trying to tell me something.

The bears love fruit. Often the orchard seems like a school for baby bears; cubs are taught life skills for the future when they are out on their own. Some bears eat fruit right off the tree, others gather the fruit then sit down and eat away one apple or one plum at a time. We have seen bears climb the tree, curl up on top and reach down to pick the apple they want to munch on. We are not too keen on their performance; the damage the bears do to fruit trees is such that some trees never recover.

CATS AT THE LAKE

Cats have been an important part of my life ever since I was a child. There were many; here I mention a few from our years at the lake. Some cats endear themselves and become part of the family. Others like to be outdoors and drop by for a visit now and then. They always remember where the food tray is located. One cat would take off in early spring and return at the first sign of winter. Come November the cat was at the door wanting in running straight to the food dish where it was months ago. The following year it would be the same thing until one year she was not to be seen again.

At one time we had 4 outdoor cats. In the carport each had a winter bed in a foam box placed upside down with a circular entrance in front. When we looked up all 4 heads would protrude from their entrances. One cold winter all 4 cats piled into one box to keep warm. When I looked inside to count the number of cats, there they were all 4 of them, hot and steamy, piled one on top of the other.

The Calico coloured cat was dropped off here one day and being low in the pecking order waited until our family of 3 cats had eaten before she dared to approach the eating area. She was the new comer and always remained last in line; she knew her place.

Photo 1: Tuffy, one of a family of 3 cats.

Photo 2: Callycat.

Photo 3: Joey, 12 years old one of the two cats we have at the lake.

Photo 4: Rosey, our 12 year old second cat goes off into the bush for the summer and returns to the comfort of the house when the weather gets nippy.

DOGS AT THE LAKE

Dogs too have played an important part in my life. While there were many the photos below showcase three that I have enjoyed at the lake.

Photo 1: Squeak and Louis at our micro electric dam. Outdoor living with lots of activity kept us both in good shape. Dog Squeak came to us as a pup and was reported to be part coyote. This I can't vouch for but based on antics observed over the years Squeak acted like one in many ways. A loyal dog that loved to round up several deer at a time, herding them to the lake shore. To escape, the deer swam across the lake. A very attentive dog to all our doings but never ventured in a vehicle or entered the house. Squeak was very much missed.

Photo 2 & 3: Dog Sandy, long passed away. Sandy was a very intelligent German Shepherd, eager to learn and easy to train. We lived in the city when we first brought Sandy up on the PGE baggage car. When that became impossible we shipped Sandy by PGE freight car in a cramped wooden box as Sandy was a big dog. He was dropped off at the unattended Mt. Currie PGE station the next day.After some 24 hours in the box with no water and no mess he was eager to see me and head for the lake.

Before the construction of the highway to Pemberton I would 4 wheel drive to the lake, a 12 to 14 hour trip. It was during such a time I was able to take Sandy to Lillooet Lake for the summer months while the family was there. Lillooet Lake kept Sandy occupied chasing bears and guarding our property. Sandy and I had a close attachment. The likes of Sandy has never been replaced even after many attempts to do so.

Photo 4 & 5: Dog Daisy was another dog of super intelligence. A very loving dog and an excellent companion. Her owners reluctantly parted with Daisy when moving to the city, knowing life in the city would be no comparison to life at the lake which Daisy enjoyed so much. She was a great companion and greatly missed when she left us at age 15. A dog's life is all too short.

ANIMALS SIGHTED AT LILLOOET LAKE

BLACK BEARS: It is an uncommon site to see a mother with three cubs as there are usually only two. They frequent our orchard looking for food and damaging the trees. Cubs are taught to climb up the fruit trees. When a large male bear appears, the mother and cubs take off at a fast pace. Males have been known to kill young males. Some bears mark their territory by leaving claw marks on trees, a post or a building. We have had a bear peering in our window. When we had a guard dog the bears were kept away. A lawyer would analyze this situation as a conflict of interest.

BEAVERS: We see beavers along the shore near where a stream enters the lake. They appear to be single families only but exhibit the normal behavior of smacking their tails to warn of danger.

COUGARS: Cougars are seen in the area as in most of British Columbia. Frank, a lake resident, was walking his dog at Strawberry Point when a cougar attacked his dog. Frank with a heavy cane was able to beat the cougar over the head until the dog was free. The bites and claw marks on the dog healed in time.

Fred Lamothe in upper gate 6 of Lillooet Lake Estates heard his dog barking in the late of night. Looking out with his flashlight in hand saw his pet dog being carried away in the mouth of a cougar.

In 1965 when my son Bruce attended school in Pemberton at age 14, he would meet the school bus at the head of the lake, leaving our 4 wheel drive vehicle parked for his return later in the day. On two occasions upon getting off the school bus and walking some distance to the vehicle, he was met with a cougar curled up on the hood of the car. The cougar took off after Bruce made considerable noise.

One winter day Carol and I were walking on the Forest Service road at the east end of the development when we came across some bones and parts of a hide in the snow. We assumed some animal had been devoured and this was the left overs. Upon our return the animal parts were missing leaving streaks of blood in the snow. Carol whispers, stay where you are and look across the road. There was a young cougar sitting on a stump blending in colour with the wood below. The cougar had eyes fixed on us. Like a house cat it could not keep its tail from twitching. I was later told the orange looking fur with brown spots was a young cougar; it was probably hiding the remains of a deer.

Late one cold and snowy night approaching gate 5 in the development I marched ahead of Carol. When Carol caught up to me she asked: "Did you hear that hissing sound coming from the bush?" I did not but have been informed this is a warning sign a cougar makes when their territory is invaded.

COYOTES: Coyotes were plentiful before the advent of the development. We frequently heard the pups howling all at the same time, and what a shrieking sound it was. My son Bruce took a liking to wildlife; driving along the Forest Service Road on his way home from school he saw a mother coyote with pups taking off from a cave in the rocks. Bruce joined the chase hoping to catch a coyote pup; the last one slipped through his hand. He heard faint yelping from inside the den. Bruce crawled in the den on hands and knees to meet up with a little fellow left behind. The place was full of bones and smelled badly. It was dark and Bruce felt around until he had a handful of fur and a weak bite. Out comes the little coyote to his new home. The pup was fed and put to bed beside Bruce for the night. Surprisingly it stayed put for the night. In the morning I had Bruce place the pup on the floor. Immediately its four legs spread out collapsing with the bodyweight. This is why he was left behind to die. Only the fittest survive in the wild. Later in the week after being well fed the little pup died.

Another coyote was found inside the doghouse It growled when I looked in. After feeding it a few wieners we were able to carry it out of the dog house. The injury appeared to be a dislocation as a result of a fight or accident. My son Bruce and his wife Lynn took the injured animal home and fed it a big ham bone. When we entered the room the coyote would protect the ham bone with its paws and growl. It too died after some time, well fed but not cured of its injury.

BOBCATS: Several bobcats were living up Cataline Creek on the property. One bobcat ventured by and thrashed the boxes of our 4 domestic cats while they were sleeping. None were killed but some injured in their leap to escape. We have bobcats come near the house sit and stare at us unconcerned. Many of us have our house cats for more than being a pet but to keep the rodent population in check. Bobcats know to hunt domestic cats as a food source.

DEER: The occasional deer visits the garden and flower beds for food. A herd of deer comes and goes above the water intake building. When my son Bruce was living at Lot-40 at the lake a deer came crashing through the large double sealed window pane on the lower floor of the house. The deer would not leave the premises even through the open door. When Bruce went to look at the deer at night with flash light in hand the animal became spooked. It would jump up and down, hitting the ceiling and landing back on its feet time and time again. Seeing the deer would not exit, Bruce provided water and feed. Talking it over with one of our workers who had experience dealing with cattle, Bruce was advised to construct an animal chute to the outside. A chute was constructed with sheets of plywood on each side. This was built around the deer. Once in the chute the deer still refused to exit. The worker, experienced in dealing with stubborn animals, tapped it on the head with a 4x4 length of lumber and out it went.

GRIZZLY BEARS: We have not seen a grizzly bear on the property; however, there has been a report of one at Joffre Creek near the head of the lake. Pilots when flying into Pemberton airport have also reported seeing these bears close to the air field.

LYNX: One day Carol and I were driving by the head of Lillooet lake where the Birkenhead River flows by. Suddenly a Lynx came scrambling down the rock wall, crossed the road, jumped into the river and swam to the delta on the other side.

MOUNTAIN GOATS: I have never seen any near Lillooet Lake, the best I can do is relate what others have told me. In 1958 when I had a local worker on site he insisted seeing mountain goats high up on the mountain across the lake. A helicopter pilot once told me that he flew over numerous mountain goats when flying over the snow peaked mountain across the lake, taking care to avoid disturbing them.

MINK: Here is an animal I know a lot about. When moving to the lake permanently in 1965 cutting off all ties with the city I wondered what enterprise I might enter into until a highway came into being. It was a mink ranch with some 2,000 mink. There are wild mink around the lake; the habit of the male mink in the wild is to have a 10 mile route along a body of water, a lake or a creek. The male deposits his scent on his route and in time meets with a female who gives birth to a litter of kits. Mating was made much easier for ranch mink. This was a job that required much skill by the rancher as care had to be taken to not overwork the males.

The photo of a mink on our beach was taken by my granddaughter Rosemary who by chance had her camera ready for the moment. This mink appears to be black in colour. If black it could be a descendant from our ranch mink. Wild brown mink when out of the water have a black appearance when wet.

MARTEN: Several marten have made their home along the lake. Al Sawchuck's cabin was the home of a marten. Al had a bird feeder out on the deck with ample seeds. The feeder had a large plate at the bottom where a marten would curl up and lie after his hearty meal and stay for a while. Mink and marten are cousins and both appear to be groggy upon wakening and take time to adjust.

MOOSE: There has been only one moose encounter and that was in 1959. The moose appeared from Strawberry Beach where it was being hunted. It left our beach to swim across the lake. I was not present but the hunters followed it across the lake by boat until it landed on the other side.

MARMOTS: Marmots are plentiful on the rocky hill side at the head of Lillooet Lake.

MICE: The mountain side is alive with mice. As the cats reduce these in numbers more mice come down to take their place. We have deer mice and the field mouse, being larger, feeds on the smaller deer mice.

MUSKRAT: Several muskrat have been cited living among the Gabien rock filled baskets on the shoreline.

PACK RATS: Commonly known as mountain rat; a nice looking rat with a bushy tail and big ears, known for taking off with one's door keys if left hanging on a nail. They have a pouch on each cheek presumably for carrying stolen treasures. It is one of the most ingenious animals, a built-in radar system that can find their way under cement foundations and through the smallest of openings. They can deflate themselves and pump up again when entering under the bottom of a door. They build multiple nests, some stocked with metal pieces like nails and house keys. Pack rats are difficult to discover when sharing your home, except for their droppings.

BLACK RATS: One year numerous black rats appeared on our lawn area. These rats burrow into the earth much like a gopher. In the garden areas they would burrow under a squash, pumpkin, or a large tomato feeding up from the bottom. When it came time to harvest the only thing left was the stem and the outer shell; all the innards had been sucked out from the bottom. I wondered if it was only our place that had these black rats but no they were reported at other locations.

OTTERS: River otter live around the lake. I have seen a mother with her young playing on the beach near URE Creek. Our early float had foam panels underneath where one otter took up residence. The dog would be on the float and the otter below would growl. We could see the otter through the openings between the deck boards, the problem was the otter chewed up all the foam and our dog barked all day at the otter family. Hugh Fisher had a similar experience at his float. The otter is a cousin to the mink.

RABBITS: During the days of our sawmill there was plenty of clover in the mill yard and rabbits would nibble away at the clover. One of our cats would kill a rabbit every few days, haul it up the sundeck post and consume the whole rabbit on the deck in one sitting. I assumed the going would get tough when only the head was left but no this too was ground up and consumed. The cats belly was as big as the rabbit had been. What was left uneaten were the four paws and stomach left open. During the winter months it was common in the development to see a galloping rabbit in the snow above gate 2.

My son Bruce driving the lake road after a day at school saw a baby rabbit sitting by the side of the road likely having lost its mother to a coyote. Bruce backed up the Jeep, opened the car door, grabbed the little fellow by the ears and placed it in the back seat. This little rabbit lived in his bedroom for weeks until I constructed a cage for it and fattened it up. When at adult size we took it to where it was found. It would be nice to know if it lived to reproduce or was another meal for a hungry coyote.

RACOONS: Racoons live along our creek and enjoy the fruit from our trees. I have seen them enter a mother cat's bed and home to her kittens and gently walk away with one kitten in its mouth as an evening snack.

 SKUNK: One time I encountered a skunk on the road by what we call gate 1 in the development. The mother skunk was crossing the road with tail up followed by her litter of baby skunks all well-disciplined marching one after the other, not concerned about our vehicle which had to wait their passing more for our benefit than that of the skunks.

PIKA: Pika are also called rock rabbit due to their large ears. There are numerous pika living among the rocks throughout the development. Pika are noted for cutting down the new garden growth soon as it is a few inches above ground; the green growth is hauled away to dry and stored as winter feed.

CHIPMUNKS: Chipmunks are plentiful but reduced in numbers due to the number of cats around.

PORCUPINE: Only two porcupines have been seen on the property. Our German Shepherd came back one day with a mouthful of quills all over his nose and head. I was not home at the time; the story goes three loggers subdued the dog with a pole across its mouth with one person holding each hind leg. The quills were pulled out barbs and all, causing a lot of bleeding. In time the wounds all healed. Later I was informed once the quills are cut in half they become deflated lessening the effect of the barbs.

WOLVES: The only time I saw a wolf was during the time in 1967 when the lake froze over and all the wild animals were sharing the same trail near the shoreline. The Game Department informed me coyote and wolf in this area have become mixed due to inter breeding.

WEASELS: There are numerous weasels around. The weasel is like a mink only smaller and more agile. When the mink ranch was in operation several would frequent the mink shed for food. They escaped the live mink trap due to their small size. Like the mink their odour is not pleasant. Weasels are known as ermine in the fur trade.

WOLVERINES: Wolverines are an animal we are all told to avoid. I encountered one and leave the details of this encounter to the story that follows.

ENCOUNTER WITH A WOLVERINE

Lillooet Lake froze completely over in the winter of 1967. The falling snow kept piling higher and higher until it reached the eaves of the roof. I managed to get to Pemberton for basic supplies. On my return trip I left early on snow shoes while surface snow was still frozen.

I was warned to watch out for wolverine when one was on snow shoes as the lack of mobility would render me vulnerable. The first mile down the lake was fine even though I could feel the strain of unused muscles. Walking down Joffre Hill at an elevation of about 100 feet I spotted an animal galloping on the trail the various animals had created during this heavy snowfall; this trail was on the lake shore. The wolverine upon seeing me came to a skidding halt.

At first I wondered what kind of animal this was. It had a small mean looking head and a yellow streak as part of its brown colouring. When it galloped the movement was much like its mink cousin. It was not a bear so must be the wolverine so much talked about.

I prepared myself for the encounter and started to remove one snow shoe, a task easier said than done. At that moment in the still air I hollered HELLO THERE to which the wolverine turned around and took off in the direction it had come. This came as a relief and I am pleased to say that I was not frightened, only concerned as to how this encounter might end.

Wolverine

67

CHAPTER 6: SERVICES AT THE LAKE

Let me share with you the dreams of many seeking a little cabin in the woods where one can go to relax and wind down in tranquil surroundings. In 1958 when we purchased the 128 acre lot with a 3/4 mile lake frontage it was no easy task getting in and out. A highway into the Pemberton area was only something one talked about. It was a train ride on the Pacific Great Eastern from North Vancouver to Mount Currie or Pemberton and a four wheel drive to our lake property over hydro access routes with parts of the road hair-raising and steep. To be sure of making the trip I carried a shovel and chainsaw at all times.

In 1973 we started a corporate development of 33 sites in what is now known as the gate 5 area. At the time there was a thirst for rural mountain property. Interested parties would come and look things over and select a site to their liking; these brave people did not seek the comforts of city living. It was an enjoyment not having hydro power and to be able to chop wood and have a blazing fire in the cabin. Years later many looked to gensets and solar power to provide the basic comforts they were accustomed to; at the time there was no hydro service and none in sight.

Our Land Use Contract was prepared and signed during the 1976/77 period covering the 33 developed sites and a further 144 sites. Road access to Vancouver became a reality. The development became even more popular and before long 152 sites had been spoken for. As time went on the site owner's priorities changed, most wanted both the little cabin in the woods but with all the comforts of home. In recent years representation has been made to Hydro for service. The committee in which we partake has a commitment for hydro to be on site within a few years.

Our family moved to the lake in 1965 leaving behind the weekly commute. To entertain ourselves we had an 8mm projector and would rent movies much as we do today for DVD's. Ham Radio provided much interaction with the outside world. With experiments down the lake we located a thin TV signal from KVOS, Bellingham, USA. We installed a TV repeater beaming this signal to our place of residence. While at times the picture was snowy, the sound was clear, keeping us informed of the outside world. This benefit involved a changing of batteries every 2 to 3 weeks for which we had willing helpers. This is a far cry from today's satellite hook-up.

Our personal hydro needs were met with our own dam and turbine installation which is still in service providing us with 12 KW of power. The photos below will provide you with more information than words can tell. We never tire of the scenic beauty of this location. A morning glance at the lake and the mountains has kept us young in body and mind. Looking back to my entrepreneurial undertakings little did I know so many others would come to share the same enjoyment.

We enjoyed the sound of rushing water in the creek nearby. Others told us we should look into generating electric power from this flow of water, and so we did. What we are displaying here is the result of years of work to get to this point of perfection.

Photo 1: The 6 inch aluminium pipeline from the dam feeding the Pelton Wheel. The second pipeline is for a smaller installation supplying power for the Heather Jean water treatment plant and entrance gate. **Photo 2:** This is the installation that supplies 12 KW of power to our office/home complex. The works are housed in a building together with a backup gasoline driven generator for periods when the service is interrupted. Further details are found in photo 3. **Photo 3:** Taken inside the building. The blue unit in the centre is the Pelton Wheel (turbine). To the left is the generator which is belt driven. The wheel is fed with two nozzles: one at the top as shown and the lower nozzle known as the Spear nozzle, adjustable for maximum performance. In front of the unit is the optional use of a shut down in the event of an interruption in RPM. Mounted on the wall are the main breaker, metering panel, distribution breakers and a transfer switch.

As of this date year 2013 we are not served by BC Hydro. Plans are in the works for the bringing in of power down the lake, but as this is in the future power is needed now to operate the local Heather Jean Properties water system. To meet this need a second mini Pelton Wheel installation has been provided.

Unlike the larger Pelton Wheel facility these works deliver a direct current to charge the batteries. The batteries in turn operate inverters delivering 115 VOLT AC to power the water system treatment works and the automated entrance gate. With battery operation we are assured of continuous power during shut down.

Photo 1: The building containing the works. **Photo 2:** Pelton Wheel and back up gas operated generator. **Photo 3:** The Direct Current Alternator is shown direct coupled to the Pelton Wheel. **Photo 4:** Inverters and meter panels. **Photo 5:** Direct drive with bearing blocks.

The provision of a dam for the storage of water that feeds a Pelton Wheel is a very important part of the generating system. A constant head of water is necessary to produce regulated power. It is an easy matter to trap water, but how do you clean out the build-up of silt in the bottom of the reservoir? How do you prevent the entry of small stones or even small animals?

If you screen the intake with holes that are small it does not take long before the suction draws leaves plugging up the screen panel. The screening has to be large enough to handle the flow of water and to prevent excessive suction, as well as have small enough openings to prevent small stones from entering. Any opening in a corner of the screen or below in the silt will result in a small animal such as a mink entering the pipeline plugging up the works. An overflow opening large enough to handle peak flows is necessary. Clean out openings at the bottom of the dam are required for washing away silt and gravel build-up.

Our dam provides 140 ft. head with 1,340 feet of 6 inch and 8 inch aluminium irrigation quality pipe. The water running in the pipe prevents freezing. However, in extreme cold conditions we suffer a drop in power which we believe is due to an ice build-up inside the walls of the pipeline; such a line would be better buried.

Photos 1, 2, & 3: Pictures of the Dam. The contours of the dam are designed to avoid the areas where there was a loss of water at the bottom and to trap all the intake water.

Photo 2: Illustrates the intake box with the screening panels and intake shut off valve.

Photo 4: Displays the overflow.

This image is of Lot-6E solar system owned by Michelle St. Pierre. We built this beautiful cabin for Michelle and installed a state of the art solar system which provides electric power to that comparable from off the grid.

The solar panels charge a bank of 48 volt batteries. The system employs a bank of 4 inverters. The top inverter is the slave providing the first 5,000 watts of power. The other 3 inverters kick in on demand each providing an additional 5,000 watts of power. The household has an electric refrigerator and freezer. A central propane heating system operates from solar power.

Photo 1: Bank of solar panels. **Photo 2:** Four inverters on the left and electrical panels. **Photo 3:** The bank of 48 volt batteries.

In 1965 when we moved to the lake permanently we thought our new surroundings would meet all of our needs. After a few months we felt the absence of going to the movies. We obtained an 8 mm projector and films to entertain ourselves. We were in good shape having a 3 KW Pelton Wheel supplying electrical power.

I operated my Ham Radio Station, communicating on the short wave bands. I tried to find a VHF Ham Repeater signal but could only find a very weak signal down the lake from Orcus Island near Bellingham, USA. I figured there must be a TV signal from the same source as there was a TV station KVOS on the same island.

I got out my portable Sony TV receiver and down the lake I went. Sure enough there was a snowy picture to be found. It was some fluke to receive a signal bounce from such a distance. The best reception was up a small hill off the road.

I purchased a TV Translator to redirect the signal to our location 2 miles up the lake. I needed 24 volts of battery power to operate this unit. I located surplus telephone shielded cable which I ran some 1,500 feet down the hill to the roadside where I could provide battery power; I had used batteries from the telephone company. I connected these up for 36 volts of power. We needed 24 volts at the transmitter site. The length of this line and the small size of wire provided the necessary voltage drop from 36 volts to 24 volts which operated the TV unit.

We enjoyed KVOS, American TV for some years which made us feel still part of the outside world. Like all other services this primitive system became redundant with the advancement of TV signals in the area.

Photo 1: Top left is the small dish I now use which provides all the TV signals we like to watch; something we only dreamed of years gone by. **Photo 2:** Delivering batteries to the side of the road to power our TV operation. Batteries had to be exchanged every 3 weeks for a freshly charged set. **Photo 3:** Up the hill, Louis setting up the TV station, poles and antennas. The unit was installed in a wooden trunk to be safe from animals. This trunk was one of many constructed for my first 1949 sales trip across Canada to Newfoundland, housing our sample radiotelephones we manufactured in Vancouver. **Photo 4:** Searching for a TV signal. An onlooker of the day would have thought this an act of insanity looking for a TV signal in such a remote area. **Photo 5:** The dish which provides our computer satellite service. Visitors with a laptop avail themselves of this service via our router signal.

FIRE CONCERNS

Our life at the lake affords us peace and tranquility; however, we cannot forget we are a distance from emergency service. The possibility of an out of control fire must always be on our minds.

Let me tell you about fires at the lake. One fire was of my own creation during my early years as a novice and not aware of the unusual circumstances I could encounter. It was late March, the month had been a sunny one drying out the layers of leaves on the ground. This event took place near the lake shore where I was contemplating installing a Pelton Wheel Generator (turbine) to produce electric power from a creek flowing nearby. I raked up the leaves on the selected building site and struck a match to the pile. It was a small fire no more than the size of a wheelbarrow. The sky was clear, the sun was shining. Suddenly the sky down the lake turned black, a fierce storm was in the making. The strong winds hit the shore and instantly spread my small fire of leaves over a wide area. So much so I could not do much about it. The fire was burning the surface of dry leaves, which were spread by the force of the wind as if the area had been covered with gasoline. One cedar tree exploded in fire due to the heat at its base.

My business at that time was radio communication. Fortunately I had just installed a short wave radiotelephone to connect with the telephone company in Vancouver, it worked when radio propagation permitted. The generator was gassed up and with luck the operator answered connecting me to the Forest Service Office in Pemberton. The phone rang at the moment Pat Gillgan had just gotten off the train from Williams Lake to assume the position of District Forester. It was a weekend and having just arrived he took a little time to understand where we were located and the status of the fire.

Pat soon arrived with a crew led by Al Staehli. The area aflame covered about 10 acres now known as the gate 1 area. Logging some years earlier had left wood debris on the ground which also started to burn. The crew and myself included constructed fire breaks with shovel in hand to no avail as the strong winds jumped the fire over the cleared area. We moved up alongside the access road constructing another fire break so the fire would not spread across the road and up the mountainside. I was distressed about lighting the fire. The Forester said it was a surface fire and before long would be all green again. Little did I know then the area would be the site of numerous summer homes once I had a subdivision in place. At that time it was a struggle to erect my own summer dwelling. For the next several days Al Staehli was on site with a back pack of water dousing the logs and stumps that kept smouldering, all while I was back in the city at work. This event was my introduction to Pat Gillgan, the new District Forester – not the type of introduction I preferred.

During the days we operated a sawmill and planer on the property, fire protection was provided by pumping water from the lake. Fire protection was so much in our minds we regularly held practice fire drills. It was during one of these days a worker drew our attention to clouds of black smoke rising from up the lake, the popular Strawberry Point picnic site. Our worker reported there was a group of young people partying throwing small canisters of propane into the fire creating black smoke and explosions. With each canister explosion the fire was spreading to neighbouring trees. We were on the verge of experiencing a major forest fire. Our mill workers at Heather Jean Properties promptly loaded into our boat a fire pump and hoses and off they went to put out the fire. Word reached the Ministry of our response which resulted in the letter of appreciation from the Minister of Forests.

APR 2 2 1999

Louis Potvin
H. J. Developments Ltd.
Box 220
Pemberton, British Columbia
V0N 2L0

Dear Mr. Potvin:

Thank you for your letter of February 20, 1999, regarding the voluntary action you took to suppress a fire at Strawberry Point. I have asked the manager of the Coastal Fire Centre, to look into this on my behalf and understand that one of his staff members has recently been in touch with you. You will be receiving payment in full for the fire suppression action taken.

Last fire season was an extremely busy year, one of the worst on record. The British Columbia Forest Service relies heavily on the assistance and cooperation of the members of the public in preventing, detecting and suppressing wildfires. If it were not for people like you, I am sure there would have been many more serious wildfires.

Thank you for putting this fire out and I hope this unfortunate oversight does not deter you from taking similar action in the future.

Sincerely,

David Zirnhelt
Minister

pc: Gary Munro, Fire Centre Manager
        Coastal Fire Centre

Ministry of Forests	Office of the Minister	Mailing Address: Parliament Buildings Victoria BC V8V 1X4

9·5H

Letter from the Ministry of Forests expressing appreciation for our putting out a fire on public land.

In earlier times fires have started within the lake development, primarily caused by camp fires left unattended. Up comes a gust of wind and the fire has spread. Some fires have been caused by guests using a friend's cabin who had not been briefed of the dangers of an unattended fire. Luckily these were not serious events. Today the Forest Service distributes far more fire information and employs far stricter regulations all well publicized and monitored.

Our Heather Jean Properties 18 site development has numerous fire hydrants throughout the area, as well as mini hydrants for a garden hose connection. Former Lot Owner retired Fire Chief Al Cleaver of the Surrey Fire Department once said during a fire drill "the need for a rapid response to a fire is necessary and every owner would do well to have a 100 ft. hose on the ready for such an event". Since that day we have been guided by his advice.

CHAPTER 7: REMAINDER

Having developed 152 sites there remained the challenge of what to do with the remainder of the land on DL-4901. Our Land Use Contract specified a lodge, office, resident and works yard for this area. This left it open to consider building additional sites at a future time. It was 1977 when the Land Use Contract was drawn up with a vision of what the future might hold.

Serious thought was given to the building of a Health and Wellness Centre. This was not acted upon due to the status of the lake road and the lack of hydro. A separate community of 18 sites was created as Heather Jean Properties Ltd.; our residence, lodge and office being one of the sites. The approvals were obtained, sites laid out with the help of Wayne Ferguson and George Miller, BCLS. A potable water system engineered by Rob Arden was installed. A second water system is provided for fire and garden hydrants. Each site received an engineered sewage disposal works for installation at a future date.

We have included images of the facilities at Heather Jean Properties. Sites in this lake shore development have proven very popular and function much like a Strata.

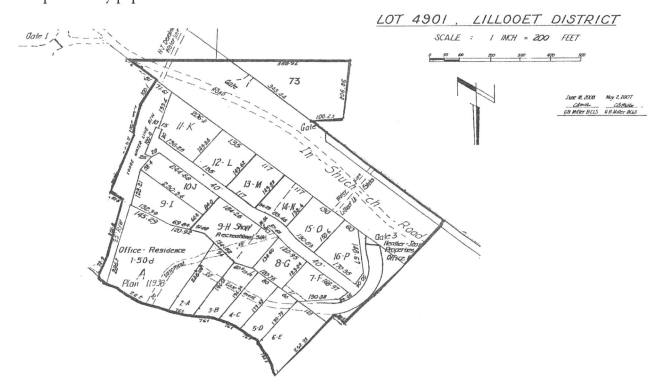

18 SITE HEATHER JEAN PROPERTIES DEVELOPMENT

The Heather Jean Properties Development is a separate 18 site package on District Lot DL- 4901. Covered by a Land Use Contract with the Squamish Lillooet Reginal District. It is separate from Lillooet Lake Estates 152 sites, which shares the same parcel of land. Facilities include a potable water system, separate water system for fire protection and watering, automated entrance gate, boat ramp, wharf, dock, picnic tables and swings. Management and maintenance provided from within. Maximum privacy assured. Operates much like a Strata.
Further information can be obtained by calling 604-698-6848 or carolou2@xplornet.com

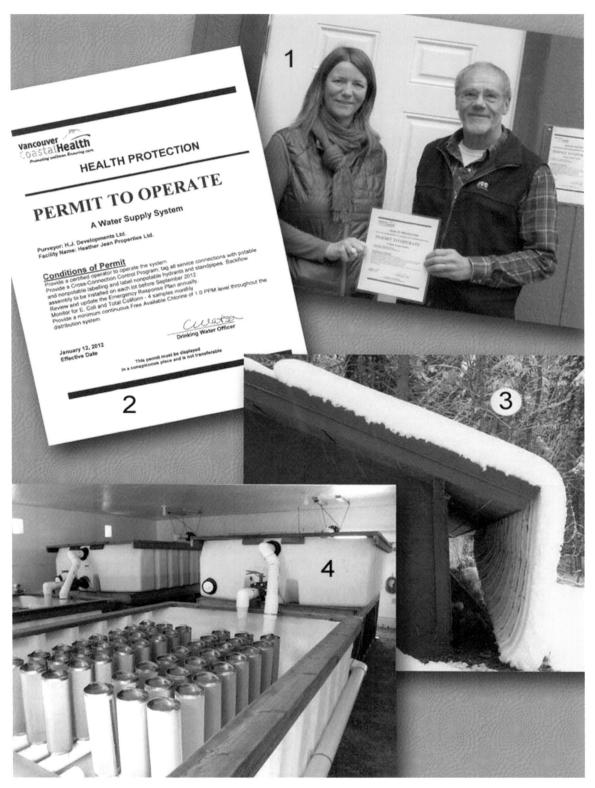

Photo 1: Cindy Watson, Drinking Water Officer of Vancouver Coastal Health presenting Eduard Klassen of HJ Developments Ltd. the operating permit for the Heather Jean Properties Potable Water System. **Photo 2:** Copy of operating permit. **Photo 3:** Snow falling off the roof of the water intake building. **Photo 4:** Filtration tanks. The intake water from an underground source enters the upper tank; debris falls to the bottom of the tank and is automatically flushed out. The 48 plug-in stainless steel cylinders have a 380 micron mesh through which water passes. The water leaving the upper tank enters the lower tank where this process of filtration is repeated. Here too there are 48 stainless steel cylinders with a 229 micron mesh. A second set of tanks and cylinders has been provided so as to have minimum shut down time during servicing periods. The filtered water is then piped out for further treatment.

Photo 1: This is the water treatment site where filtered water from the upper tanks enters for further treatment. This is accomplished by means of filters, UV Lamps and Chlorine Injection. On the upper right is the treatment building. **Photo 2:** Louis Potvin standing in front of the treatment building. **Photo 3:** Chlorine tank and injection works. **Photo 4:** Electrical panels with breaker for 300 watt electric heater. **Photo 5:** Filters on the left and UV Lamps. Not shown is a back-up propane heater for emergency use during sub-zero temperatures.

Photo 1: The Yamaha service vehicle known as the Rhino. Used for snow ploughing in winter and ground maintenance in other seasons. **Photo 2:** Swings and picnic table under Willow tree. **Photo 3:** Walkway to floating dock and folding ladder for swimmers. **Photo 4:** Wharf/Helipad with stairway to floating dock; cement boat ramp on the right. **NOTE:** All assets shown except for the Rhino are the property of the 18 Owners of Sites in Heather Jean Properties Ltd.

Here is a collage that illustrates what has transpired at Heather Jean Properties.

Photo 1: The community fire building where fire hoses and fire tools are stored. **Photo 2:** A bear looking for food behind the fire water intake building. **Photo 3:** Helicopter landing on the pad under construction. **Photo 4:** Workers Wade Emms and Danny Edmonds laying water lines.

Photo 1: Gate 3 entrance; pedestrian gate to one side. **Photos 2 & 3:** The electronics necessary to operate the gate. The gate opens and closes in response to a hand held clicker unit. When the gate is fully opened and for that moment only, one click on the control unit will lock the gate in an open position. Frozen snow and ice has to be kept clear of the bottom arm that swings when opening. The gate gets it power from the Pelton Wheel which powers the water system. No need to get out of the car on rainy or icy days.

RARE FIND, THIS IS YOUR LAKESIDE PROPERTY

HEATHER JEAN PROPERTIES

OWN YOUR OWN PIECE OF PARADISE at Lillooet Lake, just a one hour drive from Whistler and 3 hours from Vancouver. These unique lakeside properties offer easy lake access, a boat ramp, float, dock, swings, and picnic tables.

Eleven of the eighteen properties in this gated community are available to purchase.* Imagine spending your summer on the lake filled with long, sun-filled days, bluer-than-blue skies, and plenty of adventures from which to choose.

*Developed under 1977 Land Use contract with the Regional District

CHAPTER 8: GUEST APPEARANCE

This chapter is about some of those who have been part of our development at Lillooet Lake. Also included are boyhood friends who have an interesting story to tell about our chance meeting later in life. This story includes a precious second cousin as living close relatives are a thing of the past. To top it off included is a word from an admirer.

EDUARD KLASSEN

Eduard Klassen came to work for our company at Lillooet Lake some 13 years ago. Ed's skills have been an important asset in the birth of the 2012 Heather Jean Properties development of 18 sites at Lillooet Lake. Eduard was born in Paraguay, a story that can only be told by recounting how the Klassen family settled in Paraguay and then Canada. It is a story of parental sacrifice and devotion.

This is about Wilhelm Klassen, Ed's father known as Papa Klassen. He had lived in the Ukraine, Siberia and Germany where he was granted a one year stay on the understanding he emigrate abroad. Paraguay was to be their destination. There Mennonite families were welcomed as they were hard workers and an asset to the country. Papa Klassen now age 32 settled in Paraguay raising a family with his wife Valentine (Mama).

Wilhelm and Valentine, Papa and Mama Klassen.

Papa became a doctor, chemist and dentist in Paraguay. Dr. Papa Klassen had concern about the limited opportunities in Paraguay for his growing family of boys. In 1966 Doctor Klassen and family immigrated to the greener fields of Canada. Their home language was German, they spoke Spanish in Paraguay and had spoken Russian in Ukraine and were now engaged in improving their English in Canada. Dr. Klassen applied to become a Canadian doctor. The Canadian examination was in English which was a language he had not yet mastered. Aware of this short-coming Papa gave up the idea of becoming a doctor in Canada. This necessitated finding work that would meet family expenses and this he did. Not many would make the sacrifice Papa Klassen made for the betterment of the family.

Eduard age 19 and his four brothers fitted right in with Canadian culture each making a success in their new country. They now had the best of two worlds holding dual citizenship. Later in Canada sister Sophie was born.

The Klassens, five sons and daughter, Eduard, Werner, Eric, Edwin, Armand And Sophie.

One day Papa Klassen answering our advertisement appeared at our Lillooet Lake office. It was made clear to us he was looking for a retreat where his sons could purchase property and build cottages, a place for the children and future grandchildren to spend happy times together. Papa Klassen with excitement exclaimed GUT! GUT! This is the place for my family. Years later we are entertained by the numerous Klassen grandchildren motoring and visiting back and forth on the lake. Sometimes it is difficult to accept this passage of time.

The Klassens aboard the Potvin houseboat Carolou August 1990. Left to right – Louis Potvin, Judy Klassen, Mama Klassen, Papa Klassen, Eric Klassen.

It has been an honour for us to have played a part in the Klassen family history. Papa Klassen visited from time to time and corresponded as well. Due to the language barrier it was a challenge to communicate. With some written Spanish, English and sketches we made ourselves understood. It taught me you can reach the heart of a person without being able to fully communicate in the regular manner.

The former Dr. Klassen would talk about the riverboats and barges transporting goods to inland Paraguay out of Buenos Aires, the river port of entry. While on a cruise, docked in Buenos Aires for the night, I looked out the cabin porthole in the morning and to my surprise and delight was a vessel flying the Paraguayian flag (banderia) with barges ready to be transported up Rio de la Plata to Paraguay. Carol, out on deck, snapped a picture which I later mailed to Papa Klassen. This was received in excitement. Memories of the past rekindled.

MV Parana Feeder out of Asuncion.

View of Buenos Aires from the dock area.

Wilhelm Klassen, a Canadian citizen and former doctor in Paraguay, passed away at age 94. Not before making a special visit to say goodbye to an old friend realizing his time with us was about to end. Aufwierdereshen Amigo Luis he spoke on departing. He had only one regret, which was not acting on a special offer we made to him for a semi-frontage site whereby he could be near his boys, daughter and grandchildren on weekends.

Louis Potvin on the left and Wilhelm Klassen on the right.

Eduard, the eldest son and wife Liesbeth have worked with Carol and I and our company HJ Developments Ltd. for the past thirteen years. Papa Klassen left us with many handmade gifts to remember him by. The many dust pans and stools he made each with his signature knowing that someday we would be remembering him. What I cherish most is his creation of a key to unfasten a very small metal trunk given to me at age four, which meant a great deal to me. For years we could not open this little trunk. Not only did he remedy this problem he rebuilt the inside tray which as a boy I had damaged. The trunk is now in the hands of my grandson Kevin Potvin where we know it will receive the care and attention it deserves. I have held a great attachment to this little trunk. It was purchased on my fifth birthday from Woodward's store on Hastings Street in Vancouver in year 1929.

All members of the Klassen family reflect Papa's wishes that they work hard, be successful in their new home in Canada, and enjoy their family. Positive thinking brings about positive results as the Klassen family has well demonstrated.

Rob and Tamara Arden.

I am pleased to have had the opportunity of working with Louis and Carol Potvin on the development of their remaining 18 sites on Lillooet Lake. I am a professional engineer specializing in the fields of potable water supply and treatment, on site waste water treatment and dispersal. I graduated from the University of British Columbia in 1994 with a degree in Bio-Resource engineering. I ventured out on my own and was completely independent by 2002. In the summer of 2003 we (Arden Consulting Engineers Ltd) were engaged by the Potvins to identify locations for a community affluent dispersal area (septic field) to support the planned development. After 8 long years of changing regulations, provincial health authorities and more, we have finally brought the project to fruition.

The development features a state of the art community potable water treatment system to treat the drinking water from Louis' spring. The system was installed by master craftsman Ed Klassen. The installation also features an independent distribution network for non-potable water to serve fire hydrants and landscape irrigation.

I have thoroughly enjoyed working with Louis and Carol Potvin on this project and have developed a close friendship with them. I enjoy bringing my young family to the lake to visit, learn from the Potvins and reflect on the challenges we had to overcome. They are an inspiration to anyone with an entrepreneurial spirit and exemplify the value of hard work.

Gary D Young.

Gary is the retired CEO of the North Vancouver Recreation Commission. He now manages a consulting firm providing services to local and regional governments. Gary is well known for the innovation he inspires in the workplace and the field of parks, recreation and culture. He is co-creator in the CLASS software & instigator of the 2010 Olympic and Paralymic Bid for the Winter Games. He subsequently represented the City of Richmond to VANOC.

He and his wife Jill Davis moved to live at Lillooet Lake full time after the 2010 Olympics. He first served on the Lillooet Lake Estates' boards in the mid '80s and in his role as co-president the 14 sub-companies were amalgamated into the current Lillooet Lake Estates' structure. He came back to the board in 2010 and currently serves as the Vice President. His primary task with the board is to bring Hydro services to the community.

BOB PRIEST

Bob Priest.

My wife Pat and I were born in Vancouver in the 1920s both from parents who were immigrants from Great Britain. While Pat was brought up in the Kerrisdale area of Vancouver I grew up on a stump ranch on Pitt River Road in Port Coquitlam. I attended Central School along with Louis Potvin who lived not far past our house. We often walked back and forth together along the gravel road to school as we attended grades one to three until one day Louis just disappeared from my life.

After High School I worked as a deckhand, then quartermaster with the Union Steamship Line. The Union Steamships provided passenger and freight service to isolated settlements along the coast of British Columbia. When I turned 18 I joined the Royal Canadian Air Force training as a navigator.

Following the war I studied pharmacy at the University of British Columbia, met and married Pat. We moved to Penticton where three daughters were born, then to Langley where a son was born. Wanting our own business we decided on Pemberton where we could start out with minimal capital.

Pat and I were involved in all the activities of our small community: Chamber of Commerce, Legion, Lions, Fire Department and Village Council. Later, I chaired the committee to build the Pemberton Health Centre serving Pemberton, Mount Currie and Darcy.

During this time we met Louis who was settling in at Lillooet Lake and our earlier acquaintance became a friendship. When the Potvins told us of their plan to start a radio station in Squamish to serve the corridor to Pemberton we believed in its value to our citizens. Pat became an early investor in Mountain FM Radio. She also became the morning on air voice of Pemberton, reporting weather and road conditions all from her kitchen radio link at home.

We retired to the Shuswap area in British Columbia and then moved to Squamish to be near family and friends we still keep in touch with our friends Carol and Louis.

Don Wolfe.

I am Don Wolfe, age 88, and a teenage friend of Louis Potvin. At our early ages we were both bitten by the magic of radio. We experimented making old radios work again and were excited when hearing a distant broadcast station late in the evening. While experimenting we suffered more than one electrical shock and soon learned where not to touch.

Louis encouraged me to keep up my interest in the magic of radio which led to both of us enlisting in the Royal Canadian Air Force during World War Two. First we trained as wireless operators which included learning Morse code. The best operators received further training at Number One Wireless School in Montreal and the top half of the class were kept on for further training as radio technicians. We both graduated, served our country, and left the Air Force for a civilian career.

Louis and I followed separate paths in the Radio Communications industry. It was only after I retired did I come to appreciate how fortunate I had been working at a line of work that I enjoyed so much, giving me steady employment and support for my family. In my retirement years I came across a book called LOUIS' PLACE which captured my interest. I was excited to read about a time when Louis and I were teenagers. Reflecting on this I realized it was Louis' encouragement that set me upon radio as it was then called. I wanted to meet with Louis again after an absence of 70 years.

With the help of my daughter-in-law Lucie, who lives in Kansas, we were able to track Louis down at Lillooet Lake through the magic of the internet. My son Ian flew out from Kansas and together we visited Louis and his wife Carol at the lake. Upon meeting we both just carried on as if it were yesterday.

What I wanted to do was convey to Louis my heartfelt thanks for having encouraged me in the radio profession. For this I am most thankful and happy I was able to convey my appreciation in person. I am honoured to have been invited to make this Guest Appearance in Louis' current publication HOME STRETCH.

Lily Bodnar at the piano and Ted Bodnar, Lily's husband.

It is with pleasure I make a guest appearance in HOME STRETCH. Louis, my second cousin, is becoming more precious each year. We are both of French Canadian origin and have accepted our gradual assimilation into the Anglophone world.

My parents were from Quebec. On my mother's side they were hardy Alberta settlers in 1912, farming by the shores of Moose Lake, Bonnyville north east of Edmonton. My father, a survivor of the First World War studied theology in Montreal. This took him to Bonnyville as a student Presbyterian Minister, to Dr. Duclos and his Ministry of school and hospital. There my father, for twenty years, taught grades one to eight in the one room school house. This is where I attended school as did my cousin Louis in the early 1930's.

I recall my father telling of a narrow escape during the 1914/18 world war. As a young soldier his job was to transport munitions to the Belgian front by a horse drawn waggon. Upon being forewarned by the hissing sound of a large enemy shell on its way, my father sought refuge under the rear axle of the explosive laden waggon. A large boom ensued. After the clearing of the air the young soldier under the waggon looked around finding himself intact but the horses and part of the waggon missing.

Lily's parents wedding day. June 25, 1925, Englise Saint-Jean United Church, Montreal, PQ.

Lily's parents, Henri and Lucienne Bourgoin.

My mother in true French Canadian fashion supported my father's endeavours and was devoted to me and my brother Maurice. This was no easy task in the 1920's and 1930's. My father's teaching salary was set at $60.00 per month. Not having a farm to supplement his meagre income made it all that more challenging.

After graduating from grade eight at my father's school I completed my grade twelve in 1948 at the Catholic school in Bonnyville. With my father and mother's encouragement I studied piano, obtaining a degree as an Associate to the Royal Conservatory of Toronto (ARCT). I taught piano and supplemented my income working at the local bank.

In 1948 my father was offered a position as the French teacher in the neighbouring town of Glendon. It was there at a dance I met Ted Bodnar. We fell in love and married. In 1963 my father retired. My husband Ted became the Principal of the high school. Later with our children Lori and Valerie we moved back to Bonnyville.

My husband Ted was from a Ukrainian family many of whom pioneered like the French Canadians from Quebec. Ted played a key role in the amalgamation of the Catholic and Protestant Boards which made it possible for Bonnyville to have a new health facility in 1985. Ted passed away suddenly in 1987 leaving a void in my life at times difficult to bear.

I then devoted my time to my ageing parents. My father received an honorary doctorate degree (Doctor of Divinity) from the University of Alberta. His name "H. E. BOURGOIN" is the name of the new Bonnyville middle school. My father lived to 98 years and my mother to 99.

Music is my special love. I continue with the piano accompanying a senior's choir I started 15 years ago. I cherish the time I spend with my two daughters. Then I keep in touch with family members and my second cousin, Louis Potvin, who lives on Lillooet Lake near Pemberton BC.

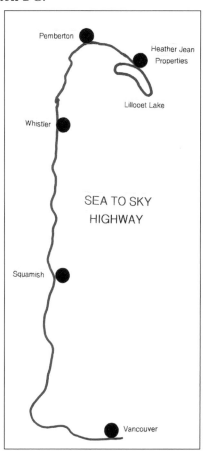

Road map, Bonnyville, Alberta.

LOUIS POTVIN SPEAKS ON HIS VISIT TO BONNYVILLE

In the fall of 2010 with three of my adult grandchildren, my wife Carol and I made the trip to Bonnyville, Alberta, the place of my birth. This was a heartfelt experience for me sharing memories of early school days and the more primitive life of days gone by.

The grandchildren Douglas, Rosemary and Kevin were intrigued visiting the now closed one room schoolhouse that remains standing and also the route I walked to school each day in freezing weather and blowing snow drifts. Viewing the land my grandfather Napoleon once cleared and farmed in 1911 after arrival from Quebec, seeing the bare land void of farm buildings and the dried up lake shore that bordered the farm was for me as if none of this had ever happened.

The pioneer farmers had petitioned for a rail extension to Bonnyville. Construction was completed in 1928. Now the line is bare of rail tracks and has become a recreational trail. In those early days it was an event to travel to Edmonton. Now it can be travelled there and back the same day. To see only a few grain elevators standing where, with horses and waggon, we delivered the grain produced on our farm was a further reminder of an era gone by.

Visiting Lily, her daughters and Moose Lake gave life to my bond with my cousin Lily and Bonnyville. Many citizens with French names were playing bingo at the hall we visited one evening. Upon learning this stranger's name was Potvin and could speak some French, several of the bingo players came forward introducing themselves. A brother had come home.

Carlayne and husband Colin aboard the Carolou, Lizzie Bay, Lillooet Lake.

Carlayne and Colin Baxter appearing above are friends we have enjoyed over the years. Carol and I had the honour of being part of their wedding ceremony. Thank you Carlayne for the nice words you had to say. Your kind words have been included below.

Louis, I have to tell you how much I enjoyed your book LOUIS' PLACE. I have endeavoured to piece together the bits of stories concerning your life that I have heard about during our brief visits together, since our introduction some 25 years ago. I must say I have admired you both and am blessed for your presence in my life. After reading this first book I feel I know you better Louis; the pieces fit more clearly in my mind and I admire you even more. I am excited and looking forward to hearing/ reading the rest of the story in HOME STRETCH.

CHAPTER 9: GRANDCHILDREN

Being a grandparent is not a position one seeks it just comes about. Together we have 12 adult grandchildren, 8 for Carol and 4 for me. Now we also have a great granddaughter Arien. Total 13. We care for them all and believe they care for us. The relationship between grandparents and grandchildren seems to be one of a natural affinity that grows over the years. Grandparents help when they can and listen to troubles and aspirations. Grandkids keep us informed about new trends and current ideas. Grandkids do not have to answer to us as they do their own parents. We are fortunate to have a more one on one relationship.

The following pages show the grandchildren today in 2013 and when they were younger. We are confident our grandchildren are off to a good start as they are workers, exhibit interest in what they undertake and above all have good characters. Now as we fade away in the Home Stretch the grandchildren continue to enrich our lives.

ROSS MARINO

Ross (age 24) is currently in his last year at Brown University studying Education. Ross' plans include earning his Master's in Elementary Education and then teaching in the New England area. A big hobby of his is taekwondo, a martial arts discipline, which takes up a lot of his free time at school. Ross plans on getting his black belt and help with the instruction on the Brown team. When Ross isn't studying or working towards his black belt, he enjoys hanging out with his friends.

Ross ready for glider adventure at Pemberton Air Field.

Ross.

Ross with sister Gillian.

Ross as a young student.

Rosemary (age 30) completed her BA in sociology and theatre from the University of British Columbia in 2006. She went on to complete her MSc in policy studies from the University of Edinburgh in the United Kingdom in 2007. After completing her MSc she received a full scholarship to conduct a PhD at the Nuffield Centre for International Health and Development at the University of Leeds in the United Kingdom. For her PhD Rosemary explored HIV/AIDS prevention policy processes in faith-based non-governmental organizations in Tanzania, spending six months collecting data in Dar es Salaam.

After completing her PhD in 2012, Rosemary worked as a Research Fellow and Teaching Fellow at the Nuffield Centre for International Health and Development, contributing to health systems and policy teaching and research. Rosemary hopes to continue to progress her career in the field of international health and development and is currently working at the University of Edinburgh as a Lecturer in Global Health Policy. When she isn't working Rosemary is a big traveller, reader, and most recently, seamstress.

PhD graduation day University of Leeds, England July 2012.

Dr Rosemary Morgan's office.

Rosemary with Nana Carol Potvin, Lillooet Lake summer or fall 2010.

Rosemary with cousin Renee Potvin.

Rosemary with mother Heather, University of British Columbia graduation 2006.

MICHAEL VIDLER

Michael (age 25) has had a fervent interest in film and storytelling from a young age, writing short narratives from his bedroom in the attic, and casting unsuspecting friends and family members to act in said narratives. He later went on to complete a degree in Digital Film and Video at the Art Institute of Vancouver. Here he produced several short films, some of which are currently being featured at film festivals in Canada. In addition to being an aspiring filmmaker he is currently working as an editor and cameraman at City TV and Omni Television in Vancouver. His plans for the future are to some day make feature length films for theatre release. As for the near future he hopes to return to school and further perfect his craft as a film maker.

Michael.

Michael with sisters Jacqueline and Marianne upon graduating from Vancouver Art Institute 2008.

Dog sledding at 100 Mile House, BC.

Younger Michael on swing at the lake.

GILLIAN MARINO

Since graduating from Brown University in 2009 with a SC.B in neuroscience, Gillian (age 27) has been working on her culinary education. Instead of attending more school or a culinary program, she decided to take her Montessori training and go out into the world and learn by experience. She's spent at least a month every year since 2009 in Italy doing farm internships and training programs, which she has organized herself. She has learned about shepherding, milking, cheesemaking, cooking, farm ownership and a bit of language on the way.

Gillian's work at home has also been culinary focused. She worked for a year as a butcher's intern and cheesemonger before taking a job as a cheesemaker for a mozzarella company, Fiore Di Nonno. Outside of work, she's been cooking and catering for friends and family. In the future she looks forward to a family business, a farm, a cafe, or a mix of the two. Right now cheese making is her passion, and she has a lot more to learn!

Gillian.

Bachelor of Neuroscience 2009.

Grandpa Lou as he is known with step-granddaughter Gillian.

Gillian and cousin Marianne.

KEVIN POTVIN

Kevin (age 30) is employed as a Longshoreman at the Vancouver docks. His training includes the operation of various machines and functioning of the docks and his goal is to work towards a management position.

Kevin has travelled to Mexico and Italy and looks forward to more travelling in the future. His passion is hockey. Over the years Kevin has played on many teams, and has even played goalie for the Swedish team in the movie Miracle, a replay of the World Cup game with the United States. In the future Kevin hopes to one day get married and settle down and have a family.

Kevin with Grandpa Louis Potvin.

Young hockey player Kevin 1994.

Kevin the wood chopper with Carol Potvin.

Kevin fishing with his dad Bruce, 1991.

Jacqueline (age 31) was an obstinate, deeply creative, and curious child. She never liked anything. She only loved and hated things. She loved books and she hated shrimp. She loved the chlorinated smell of the public swimming pool in the winter and she hated team sports, particularly soccer. She loved mountain gorillas and she hated the thought of growing old. As a young adult Jacqueline lived abroad in the Southwest United States, Mexico, Japan, Cuba, Spain, and France. She learned to speak Spanish, French and Portuguese.

She completed a Bachelor's degree in Spanish at the University of British Columbia and a Master's of Fine Arts in Creative Writing at the University of Arizona. She is now pursuing a graduate degree in Clinical Psychology. Her ideal life over the next five years would include dogs, a wrap-around porch, a house in the city with year-round Christmas lights, a husband who is either a veterinarian or a fellow writer, a couple wild-ish kids, a library filled to the brim with all her books, Italian classes, a trip to Brazil, good health, the time to do yoga every single day, and lots of summer thunderstorms. More important than the things she has done or accomplished in her life-much more important-are the things she has learned. The things she has learned can be boiled down, and were boiled down by Henry James, to three basic and most essential injunctions: "Be kind, be kind, be kind." That's all.

Jacqueline.

Jacqueline and mother Suzanne St. Pierre, 1997.

Jacqueline's early love of books.

Young Jacqueline with ice cream.

Marc (age 20) has recently completed a five month youth exchange with Canada World Youth in Mozambique and Whitehorse, Yukon. He is currently attending post-secondary and trying to keep up with his hobbies. He enjoys travelling, sparked by trips to Europe, China and Australia as a member of the Vancouver Boys Choir. He has also performed roles in productions by the Vancouver City Opera Society and the North Shore Light Opera Society. Marc spends the rest of his time at work, where he is met with new challenges every day.

Marc loves the St. Pierre family cabin and kayaking on Lillooet Lake. When there he also works in the Heather Jean office and shares his computer skills with his grandparents.

Marc.

Sidewalk constructed by Marc at Lillooet Lake.

Marc at Lillooet Lake.

Marc steering houseboat with Grandpa Lou.

Marianne (age 27) has spent much of the last several years fulfilling her desire to travel and explore diverse cultures and countries. She has been lucky enough to visit many countries, some as a volunteer worker, in South Asia, Latin America and Africa where she has met amazing people and had unforgettable experiences. This has been a great opportunity to brush up on both her French and Spanish. Marianne felt a particularly strong connection for the people, culture and country of Nepal, which marked her first solo international trip in 2007.

In 2011 Marianne completed her Master's in Public Health at Simon Fraser University with a focus on global maternal health. Since graduating she has begun her current research position at UBC where she coordinates an international project aimed at reducing maternal death and disability in low and middle income countries. This position has provided an opportunity to travel and work in a number of regions, in particular India, Nigeria and Pakistan. Although she never envisioned visiting some of these places they have all been eye opening and influential.

Marianne is happy to be back home living in beautiful Vancouver after four freezing years in Ontario. She tries to take advantage of the city by practicing yoga, paddle boarding and taking the dogs to the beach every morning.

In the future Marianne plans to continue pursuing her passion for improving the health of the world's most vulnerable populations, most notably pregnant women. She hopes to accomplish this while travelling and exploring new countries and cultures. Marianne is excited for whatever the next phase of life will bring.

Marianne.

Marianne, left to right sister Jacqueline, Marianne, brother Michael, Grandpa Lou and Nana, 2006.

Marianne steering houseboat.

Marianne on swings at Lillooet Lake.

Marianne with Dana Smith on Houseboat Carolou.

MIREILLE ST. PIERRE

Mireille (age 16) is a grade 11 student in French immersion at Moscrop Secondary School in Burnaby, British Columbia. Last winter she spent 3 months as an exchange student living with a French-speaking family in Granby Quebec.

Travels to Brazil, Belize, Guatemala and family visits to Japan have excited her interest in different cultures and languages. And travels in BC, including a family horseback trip to Potato Mountain in the Chilcotin, gave her a love of adventure. For three summers Mireille sailed as an intern aboard the Pacific Grace, a 112' tall ship owned by the Sail and Life Training Society (SALTS) in Victoria. Over three years she made a complete circumnavigation of Vancouver Island, including a visit to remote Triangle Island, 40 kilometres beyond Cape Scott and the last speck of Canadian rock before the Aleutian Islands. If she was seasick, we didn't hear about it.

Mireille's plans for the future include sailing the Mediterranean Sea, checking out the Greek Islands, exploring bookstores, pursuing her musical interests and completing her education.

Mireille with family dog Kona.

Mireille at Lillooet Lake.

Mireille helping in the kitchen.

Mireille in the snow at Lillooet Lake.

Alexander (age 24) lives in Brooklyn, NY with his long-time girlfriend Mar. Alexander grew up in Boston and went to an all-boys school just outside the city. He ended up going to Brown University to study Biology. Alexander graduated from Brown in May 2012 with a Bachelor's in Human Biology. He is not MD-bound like most people in his major, but is instead pursing education.

Currently Alexander tutors middle and high school students in Biology, Math, Chemistry, French, and standardized tests. Most of his days are spent running around Manhattan from student to student, which can be exhausting but a lot of fun. Alexander is not sure how long he is going to keep this up, eventually he would like to get a Master's in Education. He's not sure if he will move away from Brooklyn any time soon, as he and Mar really enjoy it there.

Alex in centre working at Lillooet Lake, summer 2005.

Alex.

Alex, 1994.

Alex jumping from houseboat Carolou, 2005.

RENEE MACDONALD

Since LOUIS' PLACE Renee (age 32) has moved back to the Pemberton area after 20 years of living on the British Columbia coast. Renee is married to her soul mate, a wonderful man named Donald. Together they have a beautiful daughter Arien who is eleven years old, making her grandfather, Louis Potvin, a great grandfather. Renee earned her certification as a small water system operator while at Lillooet Lake with Heather Jean Properties.

The MacDonalds
Renée, Don and Arien

Renee, 2013.

Renee and daughter Arien with Grandpa Potvin, 2008.

Renee with geese at Lillooet Lake.

Renee as a toddler.

Douglas (age 32) completed his early schooling in Pemberton and Squamish, BC. Douglas is currently in his third year at the University of Alberta in Edmonton, studying for a Bachelor of Arts with a Major in Political Science and a Minor in History. In addition he is working towards a Certificate in Peace and Post Conflict Studies and a Certificate in Globalization and Governance.

Prior to this Douglas served in the armed forces for nine years. This took him to Richelieu, Quebec for basic training and Kingston, Ontario for specialized training in Communications and Electronics. While based in Edmonton, Douglas serviced for six months in Bosnia and Herzegovina in the summer of 2002. After this he furthered his communication training in Kingston, followed by a nine month tour of Kandahar, Afghanistan. Shortly after the tour, he was promoted to the rank of Master Corporal.

After returning to Edmonton, Douglas received further special training in Hawaii, USA. In 2009 he returned to Kandahar for another seven month tour of duty, which took him to several locations in the Panjawaii District of Kandahar Province. Douglas was released from the military in September 2010 and enlisted in the Army Reserves where he is now instructing when not engaged in University studies.

Douglas received the following medals and commendations: Canadian Peacekeeping Service Medal; Non-Article Five NATO Medal; South West Asia Service Medal with Afghanistan Bar General Campaign Star; and for his work with Satellite-Radio based situation awareness systems Douglas received the Canadian Expeditionary Forces Commander Commendation. His nine years' service in the military has taught him many things: knowing one's own strength, surviving a 28 kilometre hike with a 40lb pack on your back, overcoming one's fear of descending from a helicopter on a rope, interacting with fellow soldiers and people from very different cultures and backgrounds, adapting to fast paced, high stress environments, sleeping outdoors, and above all adapt to all situations and set an example for those you have been assigned to lead. Douglas started working for the Alberta Provincial Government while completing his Bachelor's Degree.

Douglas in civvies Bonnyville, Alberta 2010 with Grandpa and cousin Lily.

Douglas one year old with birthday cake.

Master Corporal Morgan, Canadian Army, 2013.

Douglas in armoured carrier, Afghanistan.

Douglas in Afghanistan.

Arien is a busy 12 year old, she attends school in Pemberton where she enjoys math classes and playing with her friends. Arien's favourite activities are horseback riding, camping, exploring with her Mom and Dad, and running with her dog Rocky. In the future she would like to own a horse, run a marathon, and catch a sturgeon.

Arien MacDonald at Lillooet Lake, 2012.

Arien, 2012.

POEM TO: Grandpa Lou

There is a guy named Grandpa Lou,
He wrote a book and then wondered what todo.

But fate was not ready to let him rest,
As legal matters started to become a pest.

Despite his troubles he remains the man,
As he helps out his grandchildren whenever he can.

He may not cook as well as Nana,
But he gives advice as well as the Dali Lama.

He's captain of a boat called the Carolou,
And most of his grandchildren now have a tattoo.

But he's seen a lot and been around the block.
That whatever a grandchild does it does not shock

Happy (Grand) Father's Day Grandpa Lou.
We are extremely lucky to have you!

FROM: Love Rosemary 2010

Granddaughter Rosemary Poem to Grandpa, 2012.

CHAPTER 10: TRAVEL

During my business travels of years gone by, there were moments I had time on my hands in a foreign land waiting for a flight or business meeting, or occupying time at the dinner table. This time I often spent observing others around me, what they were up to and their ages. What was striking was to see well off older couples having trouble coping. They had the money to travel and enjoy themselves but no longer the capacity to do so. I made note to not make the same mistake in my life. So then and there I decided to put money aside as it was earned towards future travel. Leaving travel experiences to later in life can reduce your long anticipated enjoyment.

In this chapter I have attempted to relive some of the trips Carol and I enjoyed over the past 40 years. Some of these trips we undertook alone as a couple and several others were made with travelling companions. We have not covered all travels but enough to remind us of those exciting times, and convey to you the reader a little of the satisfaction of the adventures we have undertaken. We are happy we did so when we were younger. Now during our advancing years, our greatest excitement is being at home with members of the family.

CARIBBEAN CRUISE

Our 1979/80 trip aboard the Russian Cruise ship Kazakhstan took us to numerous ports throughout the Caribbean. This was to be a shakedown cruise in anticipation of the ship's role in transporting the American Olympic Athletes to the Moscow summer Olympics of 1980.

While at sea, I asked to visit the ship's Radio Room. The Captain said of course, just see the purser. There was considerable delay before I received word to accompany a guide to the Radio Room. Upon arriving in the reception area I was greeted by the chief operator and several junior officers standing in front of the entrances of their radio rooms. My brief glance through the doors showed banks of receivers on racks; what one would expect for a vessel of this kind.

As a friendly gesture I asked if there were any Radio Ham amateurs aboard. To which in a deep Russian accent I was informed they were professionals and not amateurs. I explained that I too was a professional and an active Radio Ham operator communicating with many Russian Radio Hams in Russia. So much for small talk.

Port of Prince, Haiti was one port of call. Many precarious small vessels came out to meet the passengers while they were still aboard ship offering all sorts of goods, including furniture. Upon going ashore we were swamped with well-spoken young men asking if we could take them back with us to Canada. The intensity and desperation of these people was overpowering and sad to witness. Later during the evening meal the passengers and crew were all shaken by their onshore experience. It was the excess wealth beside the poverty, the desperation of these people trying to make the most of our visit. The sombre mood prevailed during our meal by passengers and servers alike.

Photo 1: Haitian government building known as the palace was damaged in the last earthquake. **Photo 2:** Meeting the Captain when I asked to visit the ship's Radio Room. **Photo 3:** The cruise took us to Jamaica, Cuba, Grand Caymen, Aruba, and the Dutch Islands of Aruba and Curacao, which was like seeing a bit of Holland. **Photo 4:** Taken during a tour of the ships pilot house. The officer shown was in charge of the Bridge, the young lady the guide that accompanied us to the Radio Room. The ship's navigation room was aft of the pilot house; English well spoken and friendly at all times. The crew had been selected for this journey. The ship's entertainment director was an American of European background. The passengers said farewell to the crew disembarking at New Orleans. The crew's spark had diminished somewhat at having to unload the ship themselves. This was American payback time for the Soviet invasion of Afghanistan. It had been an enjoyable experience holidaying aboard a Russian ship.

CHILE

Carol and I flew to Valparaiso, Chile, to board a cruise ship that would take us around the Horn of South America to Rio de Janeiro. Valparaiso, Chile is an historical port, a gateway to the Pacific where Chile had interests. In the sailing ship days the Europeans used Valparaiso as a drop off location for mail and cargo on the south Pacific route. Cruising down the coastal fjords of Chile it was much like British Columbia, small ports with anxious people awaiting the ships arrival.

We booked a flight from Punta Arenas to Antarctica; the weather is suitable for flying for only a few days a month. We hit one of those bad days and had to forgo the flight. To fill in time we were taken to a windswept, grassy seaside beach where a species of Penguin burrowed into the soil for shelter, much like a gopher does in Canada. The trip around the Horn was a rough one. We could see the occasional cabin on the shoreline and wondered how anyone could survive in an area such as this. Our thoughts were of crews sailing the Horn in times gone by. With the cold weather and the rough sea, one wonders how they stood up to the hardships of the day.

Photo 1: Falkland Island shoreline. Port Stanley can be seen at a distance.

Photo 2: Taken on the main street in Port Stanley. We were bundled up as the wind was fierce. Standing on the street are the Kindrees from Squamish, BC, our travelling companions, with myself in the centre. Being a cat fancier I soon observed the Island cats had a heavy fur coat to survive the constant wind and cold. It was surprising to see children with short sleeves playing outside wind and all enjoying themselves. We visited the tourist shops and spoke our limited Spanish to find the staff were Chileans, some married to Englishmen, others came from Chile to work and others married to Argentine workers. I was on the lookout for a souvenir of the Falklands for a Radio Ham friend we were to meet in Buenos Aires, Argentina.

Just a short time had elapsed since the Falkland-Argentine war; flights in and out by-passed Argentina in favour of Santiago, Chile. The RAF had a weekly flight to London. The local museum displayed several Falkland-Argentina articles of war with their brief unfortunate history. We took a taxi ride to the outskirts of Port Stanley to view the sheep farms. Signs were everywhere warning not to enter as the fields had not been cleared of mines. They apparently counted on the sheep to clear the fields.

Photo 3: British soldiers off duty enjoying themselves at the local English style pub.

Photo 4 & 5: Taken in the most southern part of Chile and Argentina. Ushuaia is the world's southernmost city.

Photo 6: Puerto Montt, Chile, just one of the spectacular sites to be seen in southern Chile.

Photo 7: Taken at an airport outside Rio. We were booking a helicopter flight to take Carol and I and our travelling companions, the Kindrees, to fly over much of Rio de Janeiro, our last stop before flying home to Vancouver.

CHURCHILL, MANITOBA

A trip to Churchill, Manitoba to view Polar Bears and Beluga Whales is a must for fans of northern wild life. Carol and I share this interest so when our travel companions Dan and Celia Cumming mentioned Churchill it was a go! As well as being the home of bears and whales Churchill was one of the one hundred and twenty-five Mid-Canada sites I had sold communications equipment to during the USSR Cold War days. I was curious to see what was left of that endeavour.

Churchill has a number of attractions: the bears, Beluga Whales, countless migratory birds, and northern lights all appearing in their own time frame. Year round there is the historical interest of the Prince of Wales Fort at the mouth of the Churchill River built for the Hudson Bay fur trade. The abandoned military buildings and surveillance structures from the Cold War effort stand alone on the tundra.

Photo 1: Bear traps are used to trap the bears that wander into town or appear to present a danger. Captured bears are housed in the bear jail.

Photo 2: In the jail the bears are housed not fed and later helicoptered out of town and released. Many return just as quickly to Churchill where the process is repeated. Much like the black bears that frequent Lillooet Lake – trapped, taken away, only to reappear.

Photo 3: The numerous Beluga Whales. Some on the tour accepted an invitation to canoe on the river with the whales where one could pat them as they swam by.

Photo 4: The Fort. Note the Guard with rifle in hand in the upper right corner. Everywhere we went there were guards on the lookout for aggressive bears. History tells us that the British commander of the Fort raised the white flag upon seeing French vessels in the area. There must have been some party as the nobility of the day honoured each other. There was scratching on the walls of the Fort stating this was a very lonely place, windswept and an unpleasant place to be; traders longing for the day to return home.

Photo 5: At the bottom of the page is our tour group, most from Calgary employed in the oil industry. The group served a birthday cake from a renowned Churchill bakery to celebrate my 86th birthday. I was asked, to what did I attribute my longevity? Without hesitation I answered "positive thinking". The birthday party with three members of our group – travelling companion Celia, Carol, and myself – three more of our group with travelling companion Dan standing tall in the back.

Photo 6: One of the many cannons that guarded the Fort.

BRITISH COLUMBIA COASTAL REGION

For years I yearned to visit British Columbia's coastal areas again. During the war I was stationed on several up coast Air Bases while serving in the Royal Canadian Air Force. After the war I was flying regularly to numerous coastal area camps installing duplex radiotelephones connecting these remote areas with the outside world.

Photo 1: Developing our land at Lillooet Lake meant being informed about water and sewage systems. The BCWWA association provided us with opportunities to further our knowledge. One tour we attended was that of visiting several First Nation water systems. One conference took us to Prince Rupert. Also attending was our long standing friend, Leonard Andrew from the local Mount Currie Indian Nation where Leonard has served his people as Chief and Band Manager.

Photo 2: This is typical of a BC coastal log dump where logs roll into the water to be boomed up and hauled to a sawmill further down the coast. On this trip we encountered several such stops to deliver machinery, spare parts, food supplies, boom chains, and other camp necessities. It was camps such as these, both small and large, that we equipped with radio communication during the postwar period of the 1940s and 1950's when Canadian timber was at its highest demand.

Photo 3 & 4: Marine Link Tours, out of Vancouver Island, offered an opportunity to revisit several coastal areas. Their freight passenger vessel delivered supplies and heavy machinery to these isolated camps. Again we travelled with Celia and Dan Cumming from Anderson Lake.

Photo 5: Tied up at typical coastal resort. Boaters arrive, tie up for the night, and rent accommodation on shore.

Photo 6: Today one sees many fish farms along the coast. Such farms were non-existent during my time some 60 years ago. It would not be wrong to say there have been big changes in the way BC fish reaches market.

ARGENTINA

We cruised from Port Stanley in the Falklands to Buenos Aires. Before our trip I had been in contact with a Radio Ham, Oscar, who was also an ardent photographer. We were bringing camera parts he asked us to obtain for him before leaving Canada. We arranged to meet at the dock in Buenos Aires, by means of our hand held radios operating on one of the Ham Radio international frequencies.

Photo 1: On the ship's deck advising Oscar of our arrival.

Photo 2: Meeting Oscar for the first time.

Photo 3: Oscar, wife and son. The camera parts brought along were given as gifts. Oscar and family went all out to show Carol and I a good time while in Buenos Aires with our travelling companions the Kindrees.

Photo 4: The Pink Palace balcony where Eve Peron made her famous speeches.

Upon returning home to Lillooet Lake I communicated with Oscar via Ham Radio. He advised us he had on display in his radio room the Falkland flag, a souvenir I had brought back for him from the Falklands. I tried contacting Oscar again many times without success. Later through a Buenos Aires Ham Repeater station I made contact with a Ham Operator who advised his wife knew Oscar's wife. After a difficult language exchange we were told Oscar had fallen to his death from his radio tower. His Italian wife, a lawyer, and son had departed for Italy. Carol and I felt a great loss as we had made a special friend and hoped to visit Oscar and family again.

A cruise to the Mediterranean is something we all dream about. Our time had come, and off we went with the Kindrees.

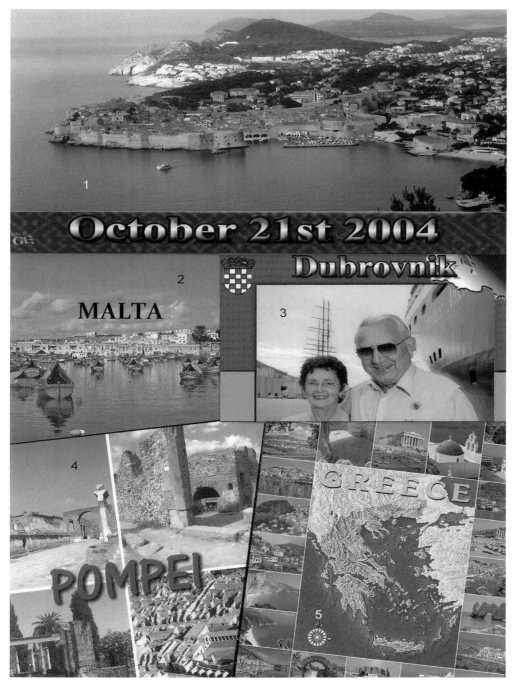

Photo 1: The walled city of Dubrovnik, Croatia, dating from the 7th Century.

Photo 2: Malta, a place full of history. Having served in the Canadian Air Force my thoughts were of World War experiences related to me of RAF fighter planes, many piloted by Canadian airmen chasing the Italian bombers out to sea.

Photo 3: Carol and I on the dock in Dubrovnik.

Photo 4: Pompeii, Italy, a buried city. In 79 AD the volcano Vesuvius erupted covering Pompeii 20 ft. deep in ash and pumice preserving the city and its life style as they were at the moment; a must see for Carol.

Photo 5: Greece, a visit to the island of Crete, the site of the first paratroop invasion ever conducted by German soldiers in World War Two. The guide pointed out the dirt air strip used by the Royal Air Force. The ancient Greek stadiums captured my interest. At the ruins of one ancient amphitheatre our guide demonstrated how the speaker's voice would have carried throughout the stadium. Our guide stood at the podium, rattled some paper, the sound greatly amplified carried to the out most corners of the open stone ruins, a gigantic parabolic. We talked about the modern applications of a parabolic reflector, applications used today in satellite dishes and communication systems. The Greek Mathematician Menaechmus in year 350-330 BC had discovered the parabolic equation thousands of years before today's TV and communication networks put this knowledge to work.

There are two exciting trips displayed in this collage. The first was in 1988 to China, Korea, Japan, back to China and then to Hong Kong – the year before events of Tiananmen Square. The second trip was to Australia and New Zealand.

Top photos: Japan and New Zealand. **Centre left:** Australia. **Centre right:** Hong Kong. **Lower left:** Korea. **Lower right:** Shanghai.

CHINA

The Chinese portion of the trip was with a group of travel agents from the USA exploring the future of tourism. The conversation among this group was far reaching as opposed to the tourist group we were with on the second part of the trip to China. The travel agents were positive and saw great potential while some in the tourist group were very negative seeing little hope of tourism in this communist country.

Arguments broke out among the tourists on this very matter. The atmosphere became more relaxed when a learned lady said: "let us keep our prejudice to ourselves and look upon this as a learning experience," while pouring herself a glass of water and dropping a tablet in the glass. My take on all this was to look at the skyline, the many building cranes telling of what was to come. An entrepreneur always sees the potential and this experience was no different.

We were shown the basics in China; something I believe is not available to tourists today. We visited Soviet style apartment buildings, their pride at that time but very wanting and dismal to our taste. Being shown the basics one became impressed with the ingenuity displayed at solving the needs of such a large population.

HONG KONG

The skyline is overwhelming in Hong Kong. Unlike most visitors my thoughts were of the poorly equipped Canadian soldiers sent to defend Hong Kong and the suffering they endured. Such thoughts are the result of being in the Canadian Air Force during the war years.

KOREA

We visited the Canadian War Cemetery in Pusan, Korea where Canadian soldiers were laid to rest; at times one wonders what for. The local fish market has an abundance of product and species not to be seen in Canada. The guide was obsessed with having us view the Red Light district.

JAPAN

The ship docked in Nagasaki; this area bursts with history. The island at the entrance to the harbour is where the Dutch ships and crews were allowed to set up shop away from the mainland population. The Russian fleet of years gone by wintered in the harbour until one winter the Japanese sank these vessels. Nagasaki is where an atomic bomb was dropped. Photos of this era are displayed at the special museum dedicated to telling the stories of the horrific bombing era. The luxurious prewar homes on the hillside remained undamaged, frozen in time with hand cranked gramophones and the gadgets of the day. The father of Carol's daughter-in-law lived outside of Nagasaki and escaped the blast. When venturing in to see what the blast was about there was only rubble to be seen in the valley, the upper hillside intact.

AUSTRALIA

On we went with our friends the Kindrees across the Tasmin Sea on one of its wilder days; the crossing so rough the marine pilot guiding us away from New Zealand was unable to leave the ship until we reached Hobart, Australia. In Australia we travelled the tourist path of historic sites and current attractions which we very much enjoyed. As a tourist you are meeting numerous new immigrants and sometimes have to seek the Australian flavour. Australians are happy, robust people and I can now appreciate why the Australian Airmen training in Canada during the World War were so outgoing.

NEW ZEALAND

Auckland was the first stop on our tour in New Zealand. As we had been told by friends at home, the New Zealand landscape of water and mountains makes one feel very much at home. A major difference for us was the focus on Antarctica and the southern hemisphere's unique wildlife population, including penguins; a difference similar to the Canadian focus on the Arctic and Polar Bears.

OTHER TRAVELS

Photo 1: While holidaying in Mexico with our friends Al Cleaver and wife Connie, we visited radio stations and fire halls. Carol and I were operating our own FM Radio Station back home and were eager to learn from others. Al Cleaver, an ex-Fire Chief, was also eager to visit his compatriots in the Mexican Fire Halls. A strong bond exists between Firemen, and this led to a warm welcome wherever we visited. Photo shown is a DJ at a small Mexican radio station.

Photo 2: This is meeting with my friend Raul Peon in Mexico City. Raul, on behalf of American Companies, introduced into Mexico the first Pizza Hut and later Kentucky Fried Chicken. Raul assisted in many of my local dealings. I was in Mexico City when his daughter Adriana was born. In later years she spent the summer with us at Lillooet Lake and in Squamish where we operated Mountain FM Radio. Adriana visited us again in the year 2011 with husband Alfredo Mena Ceballos and children Karla and Andres. A warm bond exists between us. Sadly her father passed away some years ago.

Photo 3: While my four grandkids were in their teen years, Carol and I planned a trip to Baja, Mexico as the opportunity to have them all together may not present itself again. Seated are Douglas Morgan, Kevin Potvin, Renee Potvin, Grandfather, and Rosemary Morgan.

Photo 4: In 1979 Carol and I visited Central America. While in Guatemala I was bedridden with tropical shivers. Carol took in a tour which took her to Honduras. The photo is of the border crossing between the two countries Guatemala and Honduras.

Photo 5: While travelling we encountered numerous construction sites using vertical poles as supports. How fortunate we are to be living in a country where lumber is so abundant.

Photo 6: A trip up the Mississippi River on the Mississippi Queen was a memorable experience, a taste of days gone by. The puffing of the stern wheeler with its paddles and long single cylinder drive shaft is a wonder to see. The lowering of a plank to shore was something I would keep in mind should I acquire a houseboat back home. Count Basie and his band were entertaining us on this cruise. Meeting the Count at the ship's bar I mentioned how much we enjoyed his music. He asked where we were from, to which I answered Vancouver, Canada. "Oh!" He said, "I liked the Queen E Theatre in Vancouver and the Canadian people."

GREENLAND

Carol and I tried to visit some area of interest or country every second year. Luckily with a little planning we were able to work down our list. Greenland was at the top. This was when adventure cruises were first exploring this cold, mysterious land. We booked our cruise, paid our money and the company went belly up. Credit card insurance or not we lost our money. The following season we were offered the trip at a discount as the company had reinvented itself.

However, on the way to the Canadian East Coast to pick up passengers the ship's crew went on strike due to unpaid wages. The ship returned to Europe only to be refused port facilities and was forced to unload in Gibraltar. The few passengers aboard were given a great time with the crew and ship's wine stock. We lost our second prepayment but not the clothes we were wearing. We never did make it to Greenland.

ALASKA

This was a cruise out of Vancouver sailing through inland British Columbia waters to the Alaskan Panhandle. What interested me was the early Russian presence on the coast of North America. Russian traders had established posts as far down as the west coast of California. We had visited one of the sites on an earlier trip when heading south. Sitka was the interesting port to visit on this trip as remains of the strong Russian influence can be seen.

The sight of huge glaciers calving – house sized pieces of ice dropping into the bay accompanied by sounds of tearing, breaking and splashing kept us and our fellow passengers spellbound on deck. Later Carol and I flew with another couple by helicopter to land on one of the glaciers celebrating with a glass of champagne. We were told this was the only clear flying weather in weeks.

In Seward, Alaska the large grain elevators drew my attention. There had been an experiment to grow grain inland and ship it out of this port, a shorter trip to the Asian Markets. A week later at home cruising up Lillooet Lake in our Carolou houseboat with my headphones on I hear a Radio Ham in Alaska calling CQ. This is a general call for another Ham Radio Operator to respond. I called back and to my surprise it is a fellow from Seward, Alaska. We conversed back and forth for about an hour. That is how I learned the story of the empty grain elevators and the problem of the grain crops not being up to expectation. Conversing with him was just like being there. In our exchange it was as if we were sitting together on the Carolou cruising on calm waters surrounded by our scenic mountains. This is one of the pleasures of being a licenced Radio Amateur Operator.

CRUISING UP THE COLUMBIA RIVER

Upon checking in at our hotel in Portland, Oregon, we looked out the window to see our cruise ship the Sea King moored at our door. Just a short walk and we were aboard the next morning. This trip takes us up the Columbia River through all the locks and river controls to a smaller vessel that takes us up the Snake River into the state of Idaho. The tour was to experience the Columbia River portion of the American Lewis and Clark expedition of 1803 as they explored Northwestern United States.

We were travelling with Carol's daughter Michelle from Boston with her daughter Gillian and boys Ross and Alexander soon to be age 9. To occupy the boys I was asked to teach them the Morse code. I arrived with an audio tone unit and a paddle key to send the code; the boys were to be at my state room promptly at 6:00

AM each morning with pencil and paper. They soon memorized the dots and dashes for each letter in the alphabet. It was a treat to see their eager faces in the morning having memorized and learned the previous day's lesson and eager to learn more. At the end of the cruise the boys could send and receive Morse code at a low speed. Their bright minds had already mastered this new language. The cruise ended with a visit to the Maritime Museum in Astoria, Oregon, where the boys found the code displayed on a ship's pilot house. This made their day and mine too.

SAINT LAWRENCE RIVER CRUISE

This is a Canadian cruise out of Kingston, Ontario ending in Quebec City. The ship's layout is a cozy one, the dining and entertainment area adjoining the cooking area. The compactness contributed to an enjoyable relationship with fellow passengers. After a visit to the Thousand Islands and the New York side of the lake, the ship docked at numerous historical small ports along the river to Montreal and Quebec City. We were allowed in the pilot house as we passed through the locks of this amazing St. Lawrence Seaway. Being from the west, observing the loaded foreign and Canadian ships travelling through the Seaway gave us a feel for the importance of the commerce that drives eastern Canada.

In Montreal we toured the city, stopping near the Air Force Number One Wireless School I had attended during World War Two, while serving in the Air Force. It is difficult to explain what came over me as I wondered off alone and made my way towards the former Radio School buildings. I was taken back in time remembering serving in uniform, getting married at age 18 to a student Air Woman in the nearby Presbyterian Church. Graduating had made a deep impression. Being a French Canadian from the west in this environment was stimulating. These were all pivotal events in the life of a young man now an Airman, Wireless Operator, and Radio Mechanic known as WOG-W(E)RM.

The emotional draw was powerful as I relived these moments of the past. It may be difficult to appreciate the depth of feelings that prevailed during the war years, even more so in Montreal. The Ferry Command operated a delivery service flying newly made aircraft across the Atlantic for use in the war zone. Personal feelings of "here today and gone tomorrow" speed up during war years.

HAWAII

We went off to Hawaii with George and Shirley Henry of Pemberton with their two children Michael and Michele in the year 1975. It was our first trip to the islands and theirs too. On Christmas Day we drove to the top of the mountain where cooler air prevailed to visit the satellite tracking station, a draw at that time. Off to the next island of Kauai where Carol and I stayed at Poipu Beach, George, Shirley, Michael and Michele age 3 at nearby Plantation Hale.

George and I longed for the day to see a family owned 4 wheel drive vehicle back home, these vehicles were common place here. This was a first time experience enjoying warm weather at Christmas. George having to get back to his teaching job in Pemberton departed early while Carol and I carried on visiting the other islands by small plane over rough seas. Flying over one of the Islands we could see the stone fish traps below the water level, constructed by early Island inhabitants.

Molokai, known for its leprosy colony, led us to view the zigzag donkey trail down the mountainside servicing the community. Our hearts went out to those afflicted with this disease, to be so isolated for the rest of their lives. The donkey ride down must have been frightening. Today a better understanding of this ailment has resulted in more humane care. A documentary I watched recently outlined the outstanding progress now enjoyed in this community.

Carol and I rented a car as we toured the Islands on the one lane paved roads shared with many a mongoose. We read the importation of the mongoose to rid the islands of rats resulted in a decrease in the bird population as birds eggs were sought after as a food supply.

On another Island I noticed a Radio Ham tower and Antenna in a garage with cracks between the wall boards so wide you could see through. This was a water front home and after a while I got up enough courage to knock on the door. A distinguished older man answered the door. After some small talk he informed me he was too blind to operate his Ham Radio Station, but I was free to operate the station myself. We discussed the bombing of Pearl Harbour; early one morning he heard planes overhead and out he went to see what this was all about. To his surprise he saw the rising sun on the wings of the aircraft and wasted no time reporting what he had observed. A little later another wave flew by, then came the return trip to the carrier. Some planes arriving too late to board the departing carrier had to ditch into the sea, their eternal burial ground. I did not take him up on his generous offer to operate his Ham Station as at that time reciprocal licencing between countries did not exist. We returned home reminded of the events of that day.

YUKON, CANADA

A trip to the Yukon is going back in recent history. My thoughts returned to the 1950s when I was involved in selling and setting up radiotelephone links for the then Yukon Telephone Company. The plan was to link Mayo with Whitehorse, patching into the land line service as well as other feeder links. In those days the Canadian Army conducted a service for the north in the form of telegrams. At Carcross we walked by a cabin occupied part-time by an American Radio Ham who had his American call letters displayed for identification. This appeared to be a once a year get away for serious Ham Radio Operators in the north.

Canada's Park Service employs well informed guides; it was our good fortune to meet up with one of them. Robert Service, the famed poet of the North, had spent time in Whitehorse in his younger days, writing poetry that stood the test of time. We were shown the bank where he had been employed as a teller. The cabin and lot where he lived had become a tourist attraction. It drew the tour guides attention when I mentioned the lot next door had been owned by Carol my wife. We were immediately asked what had been the price. Somewhere in the vicinity of $26.00 was the purchase price, and $106 the selling price was the answer. The guide quickly made note of this information for beefing up future tours. History tells us Robert Service served in the First World War as an ambulance attendant for the American forces. He later lived several years in France.

CUBA

In the 1990s Carol said I think I would like to see Cuba for myself, I am curious having heard you talk about your experiences and listening to your stories of the 1960s. This thinking was difficult for me after the several years of doing business in Cuba shortly after Fidel Castro took power when a knock on the door was not always a friendly one. In those days the mind set was not that of a tourist, and now to be a tourist meant some adjustment to my thinking. However, off we went for an enjoyable holiday doing all the things tourists do in Cuba.

ANTIGUA

Antigua is a beautiful island country in the Caribbean, formerly a British Colony and a Sonar listening station during the war years. We were guests of Carol's daughter Michelle and her husband. In the midst of all this beauty Carol slipped on a freshly washed tile floor damaging her ankle. Off we went to the Island's emergency centre where crutches were provided. On the return flight there was a connection to make to Boston via Puerto Rico. The enthusiastic immigration officer was determined to not let Carol pass through with the wooden crutches as they could contain hard drugs, as a result Carol hopped aboard the plane to Boston and to Vancouver where new aluminium crutches where obtained after an X-ray. It was a great trip and a new adventure meeting the friendly people of Antigua, who had little in the way of resources but were so willing to share.

PARK CITY, UTAH

This was our first experience at balloon flying. The firing up of the long flame to propel us to great heights made one wonder if this contraption was about to catch on fire. Soon we were off the ground sailing quietly looking down on those below and able to converse with them as the sound carried clearly. The basket and passengers aboard during an attempted landing were dragged over the small trees in someone's back yard.

BAJA, MEXICO

In late 1977 we were off on another trip with George and Shirley Henry of Pemberton. Carol and I drove down the coastal route with our new camper to stay overnight in San Diego. The Henrys came down by train meeting us at four in the morning with son Michael and daughter Michele. The six of us boarded the new camper and after some talk decided how we would all fit in. Michele, the youngest, would occupy the top canvas shelf. Michael would have to make do with the front seat of the car. Carol and I would occupy the bed over the roof of the pickup truck. George and Shirley would have the luxury suite below after pulling out the kitchen nook. We all enjoyed the built in plumbing, during the night stomping over each other on our way to the washroom. The camper had everything but space.

After a hearty breakfast we approached the Mexican border. Shirley was a little shocked when at the border the guard leaning back, rifle at his side waived us through into the abrupt change of scene without so much as a glance, unlike that on the American side. Before long Shirley became accustomed to the change in environment.

On the road we feasted on abalone purchased from a local cannery and expertly cooked by George on our outdoor fire. Later we camped at Bahia Concepcion Bay where George and Carol borrowed a boat to row to an anchored fishing vessel, purchasing buckets of freshly caught prawns. The best the local market could produce on Christmas day was a skinny chicken that looked liked it had suffered from dysentery. It was a great trip Baja Norte to Baja Sur, travelling the newly opened narrow highway through desert land to Cabo San Lucas.

The Henrys flew home from La Paz. Carol and I took the overnight ferry to Mazatlan. At a campsite some miles out of Mazatlan we enjoyed the daily delivery of freshly caught prawns. At the local bus stop we met another Canadian who had attended school in Bonnyville, Alberta, my birthplace. In Guadalajara we accepted an invitation from a Radio Ham I had contacted over the air waves from Canada; the hospitality was very heart warming.

We then flew to Mexico City to be with our Mexican friends the Peons. After visiting Raul Peon and family in Mexico City we started our long drive home. Each day it was colder as we moved further north, reaching snow in Oregon. We were missing sunny Mexico and our hospitable friends. Back home at Lillooet Lake I tuned in on the Ham Radio frequency in use in the Baja and enjoyed telling my fellow Hams of our recent journey.

BOSTON

Over the years Carol and I have made numerous trips to Boston to visit her daughter Michelle and family. I enjoyed the title of Grandpa Lou and had to do my stuff to earn this recognition. I attended numerous graduations at Montessori Schools, High Schools and Universities. It was a rewarding experience and one I feel privileged to have been a part of. I believe the grandchildren enjoyed my presence. The boys Alex and Ross and friend Alastair years later worked with us at Lillooet Lake during the summer, learning skills which would help them later in life. This involved handling building materials, pouring cement, using tools, running machinery, and helping in various aspects of preparing a subdivision. After they worked all day they still had energy to enjoy the lake.

CHAPTER 11: FRIENDS

Having friends and making friendships is an important part of our lives. Some of the friends I have had the pleasure of meeting are represented in Home Stretch. In my travels to other countries I have made lasting friendships. Often I feel the pangs of not being with them having weathered difficult times together. All the more so when I hear of their passing. Friendships are to be cherished, a comfort we can all use. Life experiences are never ending. Friendships make one's life enjoyable.

What is your understanding of a friend? Is it a person who upholds your name in your absence as well as in your presence? Someone you can trust? Someone you can go to in a time of need? Is it someone who is kind, helpful, is pure in their intentions, and shares mutual benevolence?

In my experience acquaintances are frequently what one refers to as a friend. Those who you once considered to be your friend may turn out not to be a friend at all. Others act as a friend as long as it benefits them. The word friend is often used where it might not rightly apply.

I enquired of my early school friend Bob Priest, now retired, how he would describe a friend. Here is what Bob had to say: "A friend looks beyond my warts and blemishes and is able to glimpse the inner me (perhaps my soul?). A friend will willingly accept my call for help at any hour, day or night, and I will try to do the same for them. A friend will respect my thoughts and beliefs and does not proselytize. A friend can span oceans and cover decades. Friendship may not be apparently constant but the thread remains."

Bob Priest and I attended Central Elementary School in Port Coquitlam, BC, grades 1 to 3, in the years 1930 to 1933. Later we met again in the 1960s when Bob and wife Pat opened Pemberton's first pharmacy. The friendship has continued over the years. Below are a few more of the friends I have made along the way.

New friendships come about in unusual circumstances. Take Willy Schuurman, for example, a Lot Owner in our community. While floating by in our Houseboat the Carolou, Willy and daughter came aboard and sailed with us.

One day Willy comes by our office and sees me at work: "You know Louis you are living in the dark ages, you need to move into the computer age" he said. I had an old Mac working on dial up. I had attended a few computer courses giving it up in favour of doing it all by hand.

The outcome: Willy, while visiting picks up the phone and ordered a computer I was in need of. The shipment arrived and with the help of Bob Eldridge, a Ham Radio local, we unpacked this new toy. Bob got it working but found it defective and in need of warranty repairs. Soon the computer was back in the office and with Bob's help and patience I was able to grasp the basics. While I am far from being proficient I now wonder how I could operate a business without a computer. Being 89 learning is not as easy as it once was. I find it hard to believe that while training in the Air Force during the war I was drilled to copy Morse code and type it at the same time.

Months later we meet Willy for lunch after which he had us in a computer store looking over Laptops. "Here is a good one for you," he says and picks out a router as well. Now I look just like any other entrepreneur going to the city with a Laptop in hand. What I enjoy best is the admiration of all the grandchildren when they visit us at the lake with their Laptop connecting into the internet via our router and private satellite feed. Thank you Willy for sprucing up this old guy. You are a friend to be appreciated.

Friendship at times awaits discovery. So it was with Ed Frazer, professional engineer. We crossed paths over the years each working on our own radio communication interests during in the 1950s and early 60s. Upon a chance meeting with Ed I was invited to accompany him to a North Shore Amateur Radio Club meeting. Ed said you live in the mountains and have to keep in touch. Being away from city life one soon loses the ease of finding your way around. Whenever I am in the city Ed picks me up for meetings for which I am appreciative. I have found it refreshing being in the loop again sharing my experience with others and listening to their experience as well.

Thank you Ed for this act of friendship, I would have lost touch with the Ham Radio fraternity if you had not extended the hand of friendship. While the art of radio communication gets more complex each year it is most satisfying being informed of these advances even though one's comprehension is limited.

Ham Radio is not just about tinkering with radio communications equipment. Today it involves those enjoying the basics in radio communication to that of an engineering level. Hams have many clubs, each dedicated to their own interests. Some are devoted to assisting in rescue work, backup communication at a time when disaster strikes. Communicating through satellites is one avenue of interest. The introduction of digital communication is another interesting phase. Hams meet other Hams throughout the world as well as at home. These exchanges have benefited many socially, technically, and in some cases in business. In my experience Ham Radio has presented me with opportunities from those I have had the pleasure of meeting. I too have had the opportunity of helping others in their pursuit of being a Ham.

We include Pauline and Joe Fong as friends we have made in Pemberton. The Fongs operate the Centennial Restaurant in Pemberton where we first made their acquaintance, a friendship that grew over the years. We have enjoyed dinner at the lake and their company aboard the Houseboat Carolou. That enjoyable day is illustrated in the four photos taken at Moon Beach, Lillooet Lake. Shown are Joe and Pauline together with Pauline's sister Queenie out for a swim with brother-in-law Joe, the year is 2007.

攝於2007年Lillooet 湖, Joe 及 Pauline Fong 夫婦在湖上暢泳。

攝於2007年Lillooet 湖 Joe 及 Pauline 的妹妹 Queenie 在湖上游泳 籃色的繩索正在把船屋"Carolou"拉上岸邊。

攝於2007年, Joe Fong 及 Louis Potvin 在 Lillooet 湖 "Carolou" 船屋上享受湖光山色。

攝於2007年 Lillooet 湖邊, Louis Potvin 邀請 Joe 及 Pauline Fong 夫婦在他的船屋作客。

CHAPTER 12: THE CAROLOU

In the early 1980s Carol and I joined family members for a houseboat holiday on the Shuswap lakes in the interior of British Columbia. We and the family were soon hooked on the experience; even our newest grandchild not yet a year old was loving it. However our immediate thoughts of having such a boat of our own on Lillooet Lake were out of the question. With the expenditure and the lack of protective year round mooring there was not a chance. The thought was filed away with other improbable dreams as we headed back to work developing our radio station.

A few years later while attending a Broadcast Convention in Penticton not far from houseboat country I felt compelled to check on the unlikely possibility of a boat we might afford. And there it was, a fixer-upper perfect for us and our lake.

Mountain FM Radio, our broadcast station in Squamish, Whistler, and Pemberton, had been sold and we had been engaged to run the business for another year. Now in 1989, we would be returning to the lake full time. And what is a lake without a boat? Or better still a houseboat with space for all to enjoy: friends, family, neighbours, grandkids, even the newest and smallest. Potential buyers of property would see and fall in love with the lake and mountains. We would travel along all 16 miles of lake, coves and beaches exploring our own ports of call.

Our new houseboat was one of five made in Edmonton and trucked to the Shuswap for rental purposes. We liked the construction as it had a 2x3 wood frame, "a penthouse" (a private sleeping and play area, great for the grandkids), bedroom, bathroom, kitchen/nook, fridge/freezer, heater, top deck and a Volvo inboard outboard motor. Unlike fancier house boats this design allowed us to make changes as one would with a cottage.

Now our big concern was how we could protect a large boat on Lillooet Lake with the varying water levels and quick, strong winds that sometimes swept down the mountain side unannounced. We chose to provide maximum safety a boat basin constructed by local workers using Gabion wire baskets filled with rocks. This involved special skills positioning our backhoe on what would be an island during the excavation period of many days. And next digging out the island as the backhoe retreated, all done in early spring's changeable weather. Surprisingly, in an area with an abundance of rocks we were searching for more to fill the baskets. Finally filled and laced securely, the lake water flowed through the rock filled baskets providing a stable separation from the lake.

When all was ready the 44 ft., 11 ft. wide load was trucked to Lillooet Lake. I met the trucker at the head of the lake as making the trip down to the launching area was a first time experience yet to be handled. The crucial section of road was about one third km long, single lane, a wall of rocks on one side and a straight drop off on the other. I drove ahead keeping in touch with the trucker by hand held radio as he followed behind. After a short distance the load was wider than the road. Kneeling down in front of the truck I waved the driver forward ever so cautiously. The trailer inched forward bit by bit one set of wheels hanging over the edge with the lake below, our houseboat inches away from scraping the rock wall on the other side.

The crisis was over once we made it to the beach at Twin One Forestry Campsite, at the boat launch 9 km down lake where our D5- Bulldozer waited to assist in the launching and to pull the truck and trailer out of the lake if necessary. One pontoon had received a small dent from a protruding bank - the only battle scar of the trip. The trucker backed the trailer into the lake. Our houseboat would not at first release itself from the trailer then suddenly it zoomed off flooding the stern and depositing water in the engine compartment. Now we had the trouble of starting the engine. Hopping into the rowboat on hand for such an event the trucker came to our help. He informed us this was the very boat he had rented on the Shuswap and to start the engine one had to know a trick or two. Engine running we were on our way to the new boat basin, tasting the excitement we were to enjoy for the next 18 years. We tied up our houseboat in its new home and admired "our catch of the day".

Four months later on July 19, 1989 family and friends who had gathered at the lake for my 65th birthday celebration voted on a name for our Houseboat. The unanimous favourite: "CAROLOU".

Photo 1: Houseboat arriving at Twin One camp site on Lillooet Lake after a long haul from Salmon Arm, BC, having survived the hazards of transporting such a wide load down the lake road.

Photo 2: Launching preparations underway on rough gravel shore. Our D5 Bulldozer on hand to pull the tractor from the lake after the launch.

Photo 3: First contact with Lillooet Lake water, stern first.

Photo 4: Houseboat tied up at its new home, a boat basin recessed from the lake to offer protection from changing lake conditions. Penthouse is assembled and the flag flying. The Carolou is ready for her maiden voyage on Lillooet Lake.

UPGRADING THE CAROLOU

My passion for "fine tuning" and improving performance inherited from Grandfather Napoleon was immediately put to work on the Carolou. The improvements made over the years were big and small, many reflecting the changing ages and interests of the family.

We replaced the Volvo engine with a Honda 90 HP outboard. This engine having a proven performance in the Honda Civic was a good choice. Now we had more efficient controls at the cockpit and the engine was more accessible for maintenance.

The fridge was replaced with a 3 way fridge/freezer unit as in motor homes. When tied up the fridge ran on shore power, and when on the lake ran from propane or 12 volt batteries. We could leave the dock with a fridge/freezer full of goodies enough for an overnight trip down the lake. The new slide was a popular addition with kids and adults. Favourite spots for adults were certain bays in Lillooet Lake where the first few feet of water is warmer than the rest of the lake. The grandkids were ready for the slide at all times.

Music on the water has a special appeal so along came a sound system. Care was taken to not disturb the pleasure of others on the lake, though on one occasion campers at Strawberry Point were in the mood and enjoyed the musical interlude with us.

A question often asked is: "how deep is the lake?" Our Depth Sounder could tell us. We learned a lot about the depth and movement of fish. The south side of the lake is the deepest area up to 450 feet deep. This is the river channel where the current flows faster.

My radio communications background encouraged me to outfit the Carolou with ample communication. We incorporated the Road Frequency and the Marine Channel. A complete Radio Ham station was installed, good for communicating throughout the world. The Radio Hams operated a boaters' net daily. Sailing vessels entering coastal waters would report in as would vessels along the British Columbia coast. Hearing a houseboat checking in on the boaters' net from inland waters was cause for interesting comment from the boaters having just crossed the Pacific Ocean. The Carolou equipped with all the vertical antenna necessary for communications pastime began to resemble a serious research vessel.

Not all the trips on the Carolou were group trips, more often than not in summer the two of us had dinner on the lake often just drifting letting the currents and breeze determine our destination or lack of one. We knew where to catch the last rays of sun as the season progressed and when and where we might catch a cutthroat for dinner. Many times the Carolou carried us home after dark, our lights the only ones to be seen on the lake.

Early on the Carolou had received an overall upgrading much needed as the life of a rental boat is a tough one. Safety features and equipment were upgraded or added. Several times we were called upon to help stranded boaters or those caught in difficulties like a sudden wind squall. As with all boats constant weathering means constant maintenance, a more difficult task for us as time went by.

Photo 1: The houseboat being hauled ashore stern first to provide access for the removal of the Volvo inboard outboard motor. Wayne Ferguson is the machine operator and Tony Shenkenfeld is assisting. **Photo 2:** Lowering of the new Honda 90 HP outboard motor; Louis on the decking looking on. **Photo 3:** Honda engine on board. Left to right: Louis, Tony Rose, Tony Shenkenfeld and Wayne Ferguson. **Photo 4:** Louis operating Ham Radio Station VE7CHN, maritime mobile on Lillooet Lake, BC, making contact with fellow Radio Hams throughout the world and locally. The boaters net met daily making contact with coastal vessels and those arriving from across the Pacific commenting on how nice it must be on a tranquil lake instead of the rolling sea. **Photo 5:** Flock of Canada Geese floating by on a log assessing work in progress.

Photo 1: Guests Margarita and Reiner Traichel from the Swiss Deli in Pemberton with Louis Potvin out for a cruise on the Carolou. **Photo 2:** We start them young, captain in training, grandson Marc St. Pierre and Grandpa Lou. **Photo 3:** Claire Eldridge, Carol Potvin and Bob Eldridge on the upper deck of the Carolou. Bob is a fellow Radio Ham from up the Pemberton Valley. **Photo 4:** Long time Pemberton residents Mayor Shirley Henry and husband George with Louis Potvin enjoying a cruise aboard the Carolou.

Photo 1: Lot Owner Isabel Hamm from Lot-37 boarding the Carolou in preparation for the wedding of her son Michael to Leah Friesen; the wedding party waiting on board. **Photo 2:** Wedding party casting off for the ceremony on the lake. Marriage commissioner Mr. Auger from Pemberton officiating. **Photo 3:** Extended Klassen family aboard the Carolou for a day on the lake. **Photo 4:** Family outing on the lake. Ross Marino, first into the water. Louis is below the slide checking out the barbeque. **Photo 5:** Another day on the lake with the growing Klassen family.

DEPARTURE OF THE CAROLOU

The time comes for all good things to come to an end. Our enjoyment of the Carolou for 18 years is no exception. Reluctantly, we decided with business winding down and our advancing years the up keep and the operation of a vessel of this size would best be in the hands of younger people.

A buyer was found, a mechanic from the Ft. McMurray area. He holds a pilot's licence and owns lake shore property nearby. With sadness we had the Carolou pulled out of the lake and loaded onto a trailer destined for its new Alberta home, Lac LaBiche, a location not far from where I was born in 1924 in Bonnyville, Alberta. Who would have thought this kid walking to school in dry snow blizzard conditions would one day be transporting his precious Carolou to a lake nearby. And so we salute you Carolou and thank you for all the pleasure you provided for all of us. Year 2007.

Photo 1: On a cool misty morning Louis watches the Carolou make her final trip down Lillooet Lake.

Photo 2: Trucker's helper and our friend and worker Danny Edmonds guides the Carolou up the ramp and onto the trailer.

Photo 3: Securing the Carolou for her long trip to Lac LaBiche, Alberta.

Photo 4: The Carolou ready to leave for another life in another lake. THANK YOU CAROLOU

CHAPTER 13: TRIBUTE TO MY MOTHER

This chapter is to pay tribute to my mother. I owe her a lot during her hard working short life. However, there are others I pay tribute to: my grandparents who I spent time with growing up; my first wife Jean, a marriage of 30 years producing daughter Heather and son Bruce who have all passed away; my wife Carol of 40 years, a partnership that has been rich and rewarding in every sense; and Carol's father, stepmother and brothers, all of whom played a part in our lives. There are many more I need to pay a tribute to; these have been mentioned throughout Home Stretch in the various chapters.

Photo 1: Mother in 1938 visiting her sister Rosa and husband George Teloski's berry farm, Haney BC.

Photo 2: Mother proud as can be with her hard earned 1937 Ford Coupe. After working long hours six days a week a drive up the Fraser Valley visiting relatives was most rewarding.

Photo 3: Mother with aunt Auxile Seguin in Steveston, BC, grandfather Napoleon's sister from Moose Lake, Bonnyville, Alberta.

My mother died at an early age leaving me with a feeling of loss and much unfinished business. I now share with you the story of her life. It is one of devotion and an inborn drive to improve one's position in life. It all began in Ripon, Quebec where she was born in 1907 given the name Alma Marcoux.

Her father Napoleon and mother Desneige lived on a strip of river land insufficient to provide for the growing family. Napoleon, my grandfather, worked in the woods as a logger to supplement the family income. Desneige, my grandmother, cooked, canned and gardened, as well as made babies as was the custom of the day.

The year is 1911 and my mother is four years of age. With the opportunity of owning land by way of a settler's grant, the family set out to Bonnyville, Alberta, 175 mile northeast of Edmonton. A rail car was loaded with the family possessions, a waggon, two oxen and the Marcoux grandparents who were born in the year 1838.

After some days on the rail line they disembarked at Vegreville, Alberta south east of Edmonton. There they unloaded the boxcar, hitched up the oxen to their waggon and followed directions to Bonnyville. The trip was not without difficulty as there were mud holes, swamps, and rivers to cross, and swarms of flies and mosquitoes to contend with in this northern prairie land. Great Grandmother had been crippled in life and was riding on a pile of hay at the back of the waggon to be as comfortable as possible on the primitive trail. During the journey, after looking to the back of the waggon to the family's horror Great Grandmother was missing. This called for turning the waggon and the stubborn oxen around and to search for Granny. Some miles down the road they found her sitting on the pile of hay that slid off the waggon.

The flies and mosquitoes were so fierce that in order to escape the torment the oxen left the road and headed into a muddy water hole. This involved unhitching the stubborn oxen and pulling the waggon out of the mud. No easy task. Finally the family arrived in Bonnyville meeting relatives who had earlier made the journey from Quebec.

With excitement the survey markers for their property were located. With the help of family members trees were felled and axed into logs. Being experienced woodsmen, buildings for the animals and family were soon erected. Mother now six years of age was exposed to what can be accomplished with hard work and a positive attitude.

With her cousins she went off to an Edmonton school home where they completed grade eight, becoming fluent in French and English. Her father Napoleon who had never learned to read and write was adamant his children receive schooling. During school breaks my mother and her cousins all returned to their Bonnyville family farms. This involved a train ride then horse drawn waggon or sleigh home to the farm. At age 16, schooling came to an end as was the custom at that time. Later, my mother called herself a nurse's aide having worked in a field hospital in the farm area. My mother gave birth to me in that same building in year 1924. First it was a farm house built by a second cousin and as the settlers community grew converted to a field hospital. I had an artist sketch this building from a photo which now hangs on my wall at the lake.

Eligible men were few in Bonnyville. My father who was the local Post Master and also the town Notary Public came courting my mother. Before her seventeenth birthday she was married and became a Potvin. Seeking greater opportunity when I was three years old the family moved to Vancouver. There my father became a detective for the Vancouver Police force. This was 1927.

In 1928 mother and father moved to Port Coquitlam near Vancouver where they could farm a little and grow vegetables in order to survive the depression that was looming. The detective position for Dad came to an end. Mother at age 22 had a large garden; most of the harvest she canned. We had a cow, pigs and chickens. In year 1930 a man came calling with a barrel of apples in his truck offering to sell the barrel full for $1.00, having just obtained these at a much lower price. This was the beginning of a business relationship which would provide an income during the depression years. Mother worked long hours six days a week for several years at the Blackburn Market in Vancouver.

Their booth sold chickens and turkeys in large quantities as well as other items. This ended my mother's marriage. My father was not of a marketing personality being born in a time when his talents were not in demand. My mother blossomed at this rewarding line of work. All through the depression years my mother earned enough to purchase a home for us. She enjoyed a late model car and money in the bank for a rainy day. Looking back it was an outstanding feat for a woman to do this in the depression days. I was left to look after myself most of the time. My mother did not have the time to be both a mother to me and be a marketing person at the same time. Perhaps this freedom and self-reliance gave me the go ahead spirit I enjoyed in my later years.

When supermarket refrigeration became popular ice cooled products could not compete in the market. At the same time my mother developed a pain in her hip and the market booth was closed. The doctors of the day offered surgery which would result in being in a wheel chair or another treatment called radiation. The radiation treatments badly burned her body resulting first in the use of a cane, and then she was bedridden for close to a year before passing away at age 40, the year being 1947.

Thanks Mom you did a great job. I thank you for the care and example you have given me. Also for being born with a veil or caul over my head. In times gone by this was considered a sign of good luck. Pieces of veil were sought by sea captains as protection against drowning as recently as the late 1800's. Sea captains vied to purchase a piece of a veil often kept in a little wooden box as can be seen displayed in the Nantucket Maritime Museum. A superstition or not it gave me confidence in dealing with the challenges of life.

Photo 1: Grandparents Desneige and Napoleon Marcoux. This photo was taken at a Maple Ridge, BC rest home when they received congratulations from the Governor General of Canada on the occasion of their 69th wedding anniversary. Napoleon was born in Chicoutimi, Quebec and homesteaded in northern Alberta in 1911. He fell in love with British Columbia and moved to the Vancouver area in the late 1940s, escaping the harsh prairie winters. Napoleon lived to age 96 and Desneige age 88. **Photo 2:** Pierre Marcoux, my Great Grandfather, seated in front of Napoleon's house at Lake Lisa, near Bonnyville, Alberta, where their farm was located. Pierre lived to the age 92. **Photo 3:** Napoleon's farm house was upgraded and moved into the town of Bonnyville where it remains today owned and occupied by another family. The house was of log construction and fitted together by hand and axe. Originally there was no centre door as shown. The entrance was to the right; a mud room enclosed the indoor well, our water supply and milk separator.

Photo 1: 1950's family gathering in Glendon, a town near Bonnyville, Alberta. Third from left is Henri Bourgoin, family member and long-time school teacher in both Bonnyville and Glendon. Next is grandfather Napoleon and grandmother Desneige.

Napoleon, always dressed well, was a successful farmer and family man who had never learned to read and write but made his way in the world with a head full of common sense. Also his characteristic frugality no doubt contributed to his success.

Photo 2: This is the trestle which in early years spanned the Birkenhead River as it flowed into Lillooet Lake, BC. The trestle was built by my second cousin Bill Seguin when he was employed as a boom man for the logging company operating in the area. It came as a surprise to me to learn when visiting Bill in 1976 with our guest Henri Bourgoin from Bonnyville, that Bill had been the builder of the trestle. We had travelled countless times over this old crossing since 1958 when we had purchased our Lillooet Lake property.

At one time a complete section of the shaky old trestle fell away. Pemberton logger Lorrie Talbot used his skill with steel cabling to pull the sections together so traffic could continue moving over the span. Many a time did I pause before venturing onto the swaying crossing while transporting loads of fuel drums in a car and trailer behind: "Do I reduce speed and crawl over the wiggly span or do I gun it and pass quickly?" Whatever I did must have been the right approach as I never ended in the lake.

Photo 3: This photo was taken in the year 2008 on the now abandoned rail bed that had crossed through my grandfather's farm in Bonnyville. With me is my grandson Douglas Morgan. Behind me to the extreme left of where I am standing is what is left of the drying up Lake Lisa where our farm buildings had been located. Most of the tree growth is gone where as a ten year old I had hunted partridge.

Photo 1: Duclos School located outside of Bonnyville, Alberta, where I attended two school grades in 1933 to 1936. The entrance door on the right was the mud room entrance. My desk was opposite one of the tall narrow windows looking out on the road observing horse drawn sleighs and waggons passing with the occasional dog team. Our teacher Henri Bourgoin had his hands full teaching grades 1 to 8 in the same class room. The older grades taught the grades below and so it went until graduation day. The upstairs of the building was the school girls' residence. The boys' residence was across the road.

In the early days the Reverend Duclos from the Edmonton Presbyterian Church was instrumental in establishing the United Church group in Bonnyville comprising Duclos School, Hospital, Church and supporting farm serving the French Canadian Homesteaders from Quebec.

Photo 2: The CNR rail station at Bonnyville, Alberta. Joe Clifford was the station agent. Being the town's telegrapher Joe knew the town's business. In his early sixties he married my young twenty one year old aunt. It was not unusual for the older widowed men in small towns to marry younger women. This marriage like many ended badly. The arrival of the train was well attended and exciting as it represented the outside world. Like the other boys I placed a copper penny on the track to have it flattened out by wheels of the train. This was years 1933 to 1936. I was somewhat different than the other boys having come from Vancouver. I had to explain the function of a street car and life in a large school.

Photo 3: This is a photo of Moose Lake located a few miles outside Bonnyville. Many of my relatives farmed along the shores of this lake. Today seeing it developed with summer homes is a sight not envisaged by the early settlers.

Not many men would take over the sole responsibilities of raising three young children on their own, especially in the early 1940s. That's what Carol's Dad, Bob, did and all four of them survived. Their Dad is now gone dying at age 89 in 1993. Raising 3 children on his own called for sacrifices not known to today's generation.

Bob was also a great supporter of the Potvin enterprises along with Carol's stepmother Maisie, who entered his life after Carol's brothers and Carol were grown and away from home. Bob loved the lake and helped out in any way he could.

Photo 1: Bob at 77 years old happily digging planting holes for fruit trees in the Potvin upper orchard. Being one of a family of 18 growing up in Southern Ireland on a rocky hillside farm, he knew rocks and how to pry them loose. Every tree has survived and thrived.

Photo 2: Carol's sister-in-law, also a Carol, and brother Bob Roycroft, both supportive of the Potvin undertakings. Bob helped at the various transmitter sites for Mountain FM Radio. Bob's wife Carol worked at the radio station introducing computer accounting new at the time.

Photo 3: Carol's brother Jake with wife Shirley. In the late 1970s Jake and Shirley purchased a lake shore site in the Lillooet Lake development. A cabin was constructed providing many years of enjoyment.

CHAPTER 14: TIME TO REFLECT

One cannot go through life taking full credit for one's accomplishments. A mentor and kind or encouraging words often play an important part. Then there is the opposite when things go wrong. It is the fault of others you might say. This type of thinking hinders one from reaching their goals. The right timing or other factors can determine the outcome of an endeavour. Recognizing these factors are what makes a successful entrepreneur.

When I started a project it was not my intention to give up when the going got tough. It has not been honey and roses, but I never gave up. An entrepreneur's goal is to treat workers fairly and encourage their best at all times, keeping an eye on the end goal. Looking back on my commercial projects, these have benefited the community as well as giving a modest return for our time and effort. This is what an entrepreneur is all about. This is what I set out to become at an early age.

The passing of my first wife Jean in 1973 after 30 years of marriage was a very difficult time for me. I was 49 years of age at the time and reasoned two thirds of my life had passed without achieving my goals. There were many more things I wanted to do.

Carol and I have been married for just under 40 years and what a great partner she has been. Together we launched the development Lillooet Lake Estates Ltd., set up a sawmill/planer mill, created sites in the Pemberton Industrial Park, and launched Mountain FM Radio. On the remainder of our land we created 18 sites known as Heather Jean Properties Ltd. My love for my wife Carol cannot be stated in one word. It has been the most fulfilling portion of my life.

THANK YOU CAROL

Together we have had adventures, disasters, and travelled close to home and far away destinations. With twelve grandchildren, one great grandchild and their diversity of interests we never run out of things to learn or at least wonder about. We feel the bedrock of our contentment is our life at the lake and those who share it with us.

In this chapter I pay tribute to past workers, mentors, friends and members of our families. Without their helping hands and the support of countless others we could not have succeeded in our endeavours.

THANK YOU ONE AND ALL

BOYHOOD DREAM

The making of an entrepreneur starts early in life. At age 13 and 14 I would stay up late at night after the local AM radio stations had gone off the air listening for stations far away. I was excited listening to these stations and recorded receiving them. Later I would send a confirmation of having received their station signal. I was part of a group called Short Wave Listeners. This was the beginning of becoming a Licenced Radio Ham.

At age 16, I installed and operated several Public Address Systems at the Vancouver PNE in year 1939. I was starting to develop a taste for speaking via the microphone. It was at that time I decided one day I would have my own Radio Broadcasting Station.

I obtained my Radio Ham Licence in 1943 during the war while in the Air Force, but could not go on air until the war was over. It was 1980 when we gave birth to Mountain FM Radio, serving Squamish, Whistler and Pemberton. A young man's dream. Never discourage a youth with interests as this interest may lead to a successful undertaking.

Mountain FM was based in Squamish, transmitting north to Whistler and Pemberton along the Sea to Sky Highway. These were small stations; after experiencing our first taste of broadcasting, expanding our coverage seemed the logical next step. We envisaged establishing a station to serve Vancouver's North Shore. The intent was to take Sea to Sky travellers all the way to their destination starting in the North Shore of Vancouver via a network of stations with local drops as required. The major problem was where to establish the transmitting site. We deemed the ideal location would be an antenna on the top of the Lions Gate Bridge. Easy to think about but convincing the authorities was another matter. After some consultation, permission was obtained for Mountain FM to use the bridge as a transmitting site.

Obtaining CRTC, the broadcast governing body, approval was another matter. The hearing went well except for the intervention of some Vancouver stations who strongly opposed our application, mostly on the grounds that a Vancouver FM licence should be granted to them instead of us. In simple terms, we were at the bottom of the pecking order. At that time there was no clear FM frequency available for a Vancouver licence. We solved the problem by moving our Squamish frequency to Vancouver and replacing it with the several allocated frequencies to the Power River area that would likely never be used. That also stirred up a lot of opposition in regards to why our application should be honoured when the Vancouver stations had been told there was no available frequency, and suddenly there was one for Mountain FM. Again the pecking order was a consideration.

At that time the CRTC had the habit of calling the unsuccessful applicant late on a Friday, and so it was the case with the Mountain FM North Shore application. A successful entrepreneur is never down, however, as there are always other endeavours to capture one's interest.

Lions Gate Bridge connecting Vancouver to the North Shore.

**Province of
British Columbia**

OFFICE OF THE MINISTER

Ministry of
Transportation
and Highways

Parliament Buildings
Victoria
British Columbia
V8V 1X4

Minister's phone:
387-3180 or 387-3181
Executive Assistants:
387-6046 or 387-6709

File No. 14-10-01/386677

'COPY

December 31, 1986

Mr. Louis H. Potvin
President
Mountain FM Radio Ltd.
Box 1989
3rd and Victoria
Squamish, British Columbia
VON 3G0

Dear Mr. Potvin:

RE: Lions' Gate Bridge No. 1481
    F.M. Broadcasting Licence

Reference is to your letter of November 24, 1986, to John Reynolds,
M.L.A., regarding your application for an F.M. broadcasting licence.

As noted in the letter of March 18, 1985, from my predecessor, the
antenna could be located at the top of the north main tower of the Lions'
Gate Bridge and the broadcast transmitter could be located between the
legs of the north main tower. These locations remain acceptable in
principle to my Ministry.

Yours truly,

Cliff Michael
Minister

cc: Mr. John Reynolds, M.L.A.,
     West Vancouver-Howe Sound

Letter from the Ministry of Highways; approval for the use of the North Tower Lions Gate Bridge.

I owe much to my wife Carol. At age 49 when my first wife Jean passed away I did not believe a happy productive life would be in the future. But here we are some 40 years later enjoying life together at Lillooet Lake, such as cruising aboard the houseboat Carolou.

There was more fun to be had, however. Carol encouraged me to get back into Ham Radio, and so I did both on the Carolou and at home. In my earlier days as a radio technician I equipped many vessels and aircraft with radio communications equipment. It was work I very much enjoyed and more so when hearing these vessels and aircraft communicating from faraway places. It is a thrill for a radio enthusiast. It is something you have created that did not exist before. I had a Ham Radio installation in 1945 long before operating VE7CHN aboard the Carolou, contacting many Ham Radio operators around the world and locally as well.

The time to do these things in life is when you are still active. At age 89 it is all water under the bridge, or in our case water under the pontoons. Carol and I often talk about our commercial radio broadcasting days, our travels and tranquil house boating days, happy that we had seized the opportunity to create the powerful memories we now enjoy in our later years.

This next image is the culmination of my early life's dream of owning a boat on a lake. Planning and good fortune play a part in one's life and so it is with our houseboat on Lillooet Lake.

Louis and Carol Potvin on the upper deck of the houseboat Carolou.

Photo 1: Relaxing at the wheel of the Houseboat Carolou, enjoying the tranquillity of the lake; monitoring the lake bottom on the depth finder with a fish or two appearing on the display. Behind is the Radio Ham station that keeps me in touch with friends and contacts across the world. **Photo 2:** Outside on deck is my wife and First Mate Carol, a capable deck hand and welcoming committee when we have guests aboard. **Photo 3:** A beautiful sunrise, every season brings its own outstanding displays of beauty.

This image is of my two children Heather and Bruce who have passed away and the four children they raised. My wife Carol with warmth and devotion provided the loving relationship in this family situation, their maternal grandmother having passed away years earlier in 1973.

Photo 1: The four grandchildren shown are Renee and Kevin who are on each side of their cousin Douglas (centre), and lower right is Rosemary. Douglas and Rosemary are my daughter Heather's two children. Taken in 1988 at Swanson Creek where Bruce and wife Lynn were obtaining logs for their sawmill Creekside Forest Products Ltd. **Photo 2:** My daughter Heather's pride and joy, daughter Rosemary and son Douglas. **Photo 3:** Taken on Boxing Day year 2008, at Lillooet Lake. From left to right are Douglas Morgan, sister Rosemary Morgan, cousins Renee and Kevin Potvin. **Photo 4:** Taken at the Gold Pan campsite in the Fraser Canyon in year 1955. These are my two children, Heather age 6 and on the left her brother Bruce age 4. They were a lovely pair of kids as you can see from their happy faces. They brought great joy to their mother and I. **Photo 5:** Years later Bruce my son with his two children Kevin and Renee. **Photo 6:** On board the Carolou. Shown are 3 generations of Potvins: grandson Kevin, son Bruce and grandfather Louis.

The next images are of photos of Carol's family.

Photo 1 & 2: Carol's Dad Bob and Stepmother Maisie in 1980.
Photo 3: Carol's younger brother Jake always with a happy smile.
Photo 4: Bob Roycroft, Carol's dad, his youthful looks set him apart until his passing in 1993.

Photo 1: Carol and daughters ready for a special event. Michelle St. Pierre on the left and Suzanne St. Pierre on the right. **Photo 2:** Photo taken when visiting Carol's mother in Ocean Falls on the BC coast. Circa 1965, Suzanne, Michelle and Carol's mother Millie. **Photo 3:** Late fall morning in Lynn Valley, North Vancouver, Carol's children, Paul, Michelle and Suzanne ready for school. **Photo 4:** Daughter Michelle, from Boston visiting family in Vancouver. **Photo 5:** Carol's daughter Suzanne. **Photo 6:** Paul, Carol's son, at Lillooet Lake with our dog Daisy.

The following images are of past workers, mentors, and friends.

Top Photo: Kurt Poetzschke. Kurt purchased a site in our Heather Jean Development in the early 1970s. Only the hardy with a vision contemplated such an undertaking. Kurt was one of those people. A friendship developed and before long Kurt and Marlene had a cabin up and ready for their young children Brian and Lisa. Kurt has been a steady hand in the development.

In preparing Home Stretch we drew on Kurt's skills as a commercial artist. The collages you see throughout this book are of his creation. It has been wonderful for us to have had his professional help in completing this project.

Photo 2: Eve Alvarez. Carol and I met Eve while holidaying in Guatemala, Central America. We were staying at a small hotel and began conversing with the desk clerk, a bright young man studying law. Our conversation took us to the difficulties we were having employing a cook for the mill crew working on site at Lillooet Lake. The young man said he knew a lady who would be suitable for that position and called her for an interview. It was difficult meeting with our limited Spanish and her few words of English.

Not only did Eve complete her first tour, she came back for a second engagement. This is an example where mutual trust overrides when common sense tells you to "beware". Years later we met Eve again in Los Angeles, California, when we were attending a radio broadcasting convention.

Photo 3: Gary Moe. We first met Gary in the 1970s when he operated a log unloading machine at the long defunct Evan's Mill in Pemberton. One bite of this machine and a truck load of logs were deposited on the feed line to the saws where my son Bruce was a sawyer. You could tell that Gary had the entrepreneurial spirit in him and was going places. He married Susan, the first office worker for the Squamish Lillooet Regional District under whose by-laws our companies operate.

Gary now many years later owns and operates several auto dealerships in Red Deer, Alberta. His companies are some of the major employers in town. At age 63, Gary and wife Susan still have many more years left to further exercise their potent entrepreneurial spirit. Gary was one of the first to purchase a lake shore site now part of Lillooet Lake Estates Ltd.

Photo 4: Jacques Morel. I first made contact with Jacques over Ham Radio internet. Jacques resides in Quebec City and is a Toxicologist. I soon discovered Jacques knew well where we lived, as he frequently visited his daughter Natalie in nearby Pemberton. Later we had the pleasure of taking Jacques and his wife Pat on a Lillooet Lake houseboat cruise. My early language being French, it did not take long for our friendship to flourish.

Later Carol and I travelled on a cruise out of New Jersey through American Acadia ending in Quebec City. There we met Jacques and Pat for a unique sightseeing trip around the city and countryside, making our stay most enjoyable. The connection to such friendships is Ham Radio.

Bottom Photo: George Merchant. George has accomplished much in life equipped as he is with a drive to create things. His interest in radio carried him into broadcasting as an engineer, studio designer of Radio and TV stations. A man of many talents, George's contribution to Ham Radio has been immense. George was a co-pilot with twin engine experience, and was successful in marketing with his degree in Business Administration. He is a dedicated family man and a very pleasant friend. My technical knowledge expands every time I meet George.

Photo 1: Wayne Ferguson. Wayne worked for Heather Jean Properties on and off over a period of 20 years. This covered services as a machine operator, laying of water lines, repairing equipment, and preparing sites. Later he assisted in the difficult tasks in setting up the Mountain FM Radio Towers. Whenever the going got difficult Wayne was the person you could count on. Circa 1974 to 2004.

Photo 2: Chris Malthaner. This photo is one of the younger residents of the Lake Community. Chris is a talented builder and faller. Trees are fast growing at the lake so Chris is often called upon for control measures. Here he is shown climbing a tree he is about to fall section at a time in a very crowded area. Chris and his wife Christiane have two boys who travel to Pemberton for school each day.

Photo 3: Brian Antonson. Carol and I first met Brian when he was an instructor at the BC Institute of Technology (BCIT) teaching Radio Broadcasting and we owned and operated Mountain FM Radio. The school provided the students who did their practicum at our station. It was with much pleasure we met Brian again at a Ham Radio gathering at the Burnaby Museum early in 2013.

Photo 4: Angus Jones. Angus joined the Heather Jean Properties building crew at Lillooet Lake in the early 1980s. He was very much missed when he moved on to Whistler for more regular work. Later Angus became a court worker and advocate for the Mount Currie community.

Photo 5: Tony Shenkenfeld. Tony was our builder at Heather Jean Properties during the late 1970s and 1980s at Lillooet Lake. Several upscale cabins were constructed during that time. When our building projects were completed Tony returned to Vancouver Island to teach at a vocational School, and later going back to building construction, his first love.

CHAPTER 15: RETIREMENT

Photo 1: Rainbow over the lake.
Photo 2: Grandpa with 89 year celebration cake.
Photo 3: Sunrise over the lake.

Now July in 2013 I can say I am going on 90. Having lived this long has been a gift, life has brought me great satisfaction. My grandfather lived to age 96 and his father to 92. Being of French Canadian heritage gave me comfort in both our English and French cultures. Exposure to a second language as a youth has made it easier to pick up unfamiliar languages. This was of great use to me while conducting business in Spanish speaking countries.

I am asked the secret to a long life. I believe leading a balanced life, keeping a positive outlook and laughing a lot contributes to wellbeing as does what you consume. Plan for holiday time before old age takes its toll. Work towards fulfilling your dreams. It is best when the wind blows with you and you have the good fortune of support from family and friends.

My entrepreneurial drive has driven me most of my life. This inner push to create I believe you are born with and grows as life goes on. At age 16, I started as a radio repair man. This led me to serve in the Royal Canadian Air Force during the war as a Wireless Operator/Radio Mechanic. After being discharged I was fortunate to be given a job as a radio technician with a small company. Over a period of 18 years the company expanded under my function as Managing Director. This took me across Canada, the USA, Japan, Cuba, and South America.

I believe our dream for the future of Lillooet Lake when it was raw unorganized territory with limited access was influenced by my forefathers who came from Quebec as homesteaders to northern Alberta around 1911. They never gave up against difficult circumstances and neither have I. Our undertakings have affected many people creating employment and opportunity often for those just beginning their working life.

I extend a great thank-you to all who gave me the opportunity to develop my passion to create. A special thank-you to my wife Carol, who has worked alongside me in all our undertakings.

Louis H. Potvin

CPSIA information can be obtained at www.ICGtesting.com
Printed in the USA
BVIW12n1307010915
415666BV00001B/1